IN GOD WE TRUST

A Bible Study About Money

Desmond A. Douglas

CONTENTS

PREFACE

As a minister of the Gospel and a licensed financial advisor, it was only a matter of time before I combined these two vital components of my life. It wasn't until I committed to do this study for my church that I realized the financial practicalities of the Bible.

Most people spend more time planning their next vacation than their financial future. My mission is to educate, empower and encourage all who are serious about learning and applying what God has to say about this dynamic topic.

Without any complicated formulas, fancy candlestick charts or excel spreadsheets, my intention is to reveal the scriptures pertaining to money, wealth, and possessions, and extract the principles that can immediately be put into practice.

INTRODUCTION

There are over 2,350 scriptures associated with wealth, including money and possessions. There are 700 scriptures with direct reference to money. Money was one of Jesus' most talked about topics in the Bible. In fact, sixteen out of thirty-eight parables have some reference to money (or handling of possessions). Amongst those parables that reference money, there are more verses about "giving" than any other subject about money.

The Bible refers to principles concerning money- not laws. Although there is no punishment for disobedience, we cannot simply use scripture as our financial resolution without adherence to these principles. Everyone has their own unique experience with money. Nevertheless, as we gain understanding on how to handle God's resources, we realize obedience and discipline are prerequisites.

What is money?

Money is a medium of exchange, it's neither good nor bad. It can be measured by ownership of possessions, intellectual/creative property, etc. Money is also based on intrinsic value, or trust by way of credit. It can be used for charity, education, health care, as well as funding terrorism, prostitution, illegal drugs and guns. When we look at what drives us to possess money, the means in which we earn money, or how we go about managing money, it tells the true story of our heart.

Being that God doesn't personally need money, how do you feel God uses money for His purpose and glory?

Money can be used as a tool to train us and as a mirror to help us reflect where we are spiritually. Money becomes evil when we separate the "provision" from the "Provider." It's easy to understand how God owns it all. We confess that God is the ruler of our lives, but in the area of finance we allow our personal desires to override God's direction. Rarely do most consult with the Holy Spirit on how to manage His assets.

Do you consult with God when managing His assets?

Does God get glory out of you living in financial abundance, mediocrity, or lack?

A. THE SOURCE OF MONEY

1. HE OWNS IT ALL

Yours, O Lord, is the greatness and the power and the glory and the victory and the majesty, indeed everything that is in the heavens and the earth; Yours is the dominion, O Lord, and You exalt Yourself as head overall. Both riches and honor come from You, and You rule overall, and in Your hand is power and might; and it lies in Your hand to make great and to strengthen everyone. 1 Chronicles 29:11-12

As King David gave his wealth toward the building of this magnificent temple, he acknowledges God's greatness, power, glory, victory, and majesty. He recognizes God as the source of all he is, and all he has.

There is nothing in this world that we could give God that He doesn't already own. What He wants is our genuine heartfelt love, and fellowship.

The earth is the Lord's, and all it contains, the world, and those who dwell in it. For He has founded it upon the seas and established it upon the rivers. Psalm 24:1-2

In *Psalm 50:10,* it states

> *for every animal of the forest is mine, and the cattle on a thousand hills. I know every bird in the mountains, and the insects in the fields are mine.*

These scriptures tell us that the earth and all that is within the earth, including those who dwell in it, belongs to the Lord. In today's terms, this translates to every unit of land, air, and sea, from hard commodities (gold, silver, rubber, oil, diamonds) to soft commodities (beef, chickens, corn, wheat, sugar, coffee). Anything and everything that we can imagine, all belongs to, and originates from- God!

God's also the source of our talents, inventions, creativity, and our wisdom. In fact, He had to remind the Israelites,

> *you may say in your heart, 'My power and the strength of my hand made me this wealth.' But you shall remember the Lord your God, for it is He who is giving you power to make wealth, that He may confirm His covenant which He swore to your fathers, as it is this day. Deuteronomy 8:17-18*

God provided for Israel in the wilderness, giving them manna to eat in the desert and produced water from a hard rock. He is the Source, yet He's interested in a covenant with us, to love and to fellowship with him.

How special is that to you?

What makes us rich in God's eyes?

> *It is the blessing of the Lord that makes rich, And He adds*

no sorrow to it. Proverbs 10:22

How do we receive the blessing of the Lord?

By relationship and covenant.

> *"And my God will meet all your needs according to his glorious riches in Christ Jesus." Philippians 4:19*

Paul spoke of God's provision through gifts sent to him by the Philippians that helped him in his ministry. As his needs were supplied, he extended the blessing by saying Phil 4:19.

God is the Provider, with the provision. He says in Matthew, seek ye first the Kingdom of God and his righteousness and all these things will be added to you. All God wants is relationship and fellowship. He wants us to seek him in all things, and what we need he will provide.

God provided for Paul through the Philippians. Paul told the Philippians, because they gave to him, God would also be their source in time of need. In the Parable about worry, Jesus teaches us not to stress out.

> *'What will we eat?' or 'What will we drink?' or 'What will we wear for clothing?' For the Gentiles eagerly seek all these things; for your heavenly Father knows that you need all these things. But seek first His kingdom and His righteousness, and all these things will be added to you. Matthew 6:31-33*

He owns it all, and we must trust that He knows how to get it to us. The reason money is mentioned so much in the bible is because our daily lives are so impacted by money.

How is your daily life impacted by money?

We work 9 to 5 for our money, we establish our homes and businesses and even social circles based around money. We acquire possessions directly connected to our personal desires, because we are emotionally attached to the possessions that our money buys. Our hearts are involved in our spending habits. It's a literal reflection of what we value. The issue arises when we ignore God's direction to pursue our personal desires.

This is why money has the potential to interfere in our relationship with God. When we recognize God as our Source, we are declaring allegiance with the "Provider," over the "provision." It is impossible to choose both.

> *No one can serve two masters. Either he will hate the one and love the other, or he will be devoted to one and despise the other. You cannot serve God and wealth. Matthew 6:24*

We are challenged with a decision to choose God over money. The temptation to follow selfish ambition over the leading of the Holy Spirit happens every day to everyone on every level of life. As we trust God to guide us through our lives, we must recognize daily that all in this world is His, and He allows us to partake in the management of a portion of His resources. How we manage that portion (through our relationship with Him) will determine how God trusts us in other areas.

Do you think that God tests us by our use of money?

What can be revealed by the way we manage money?

I don't believe most people have an issue recognizing that God is the ultimate source of all wealth, but I think the issue arises when we don't allow Him to be Lord in the area of our finances. If we took the perspective that God owns it all, and we are simply managers/stewards, then we don't have to carry the daily stress when earning, maintaining, and protecting the money we have. Our cares are cast on Jehovah Jireh, our Provider because he produces wealth through us. We are simply conduits that allow money to pass, and as the provider, he makes sure were given the provision necessary to live.

Key Takeaways:

1. Everything in heaven and earth belongs to God and comes from God.

2. He expects us to have fellowship with him, using our skills and talents to produce wealth.

3. If we trust Him, and allow the Holy Spirit to guide us, He will become the provider we need.

4. Money is simply a tool but can be used for good and evil purposes. There is an emotional attachment to our money because it buys the possessions we desire. Therefore, a conflict is formed in our hearts.

5. We must choose daily who we will serve.

2. THE UNCERTAINTY OF MONEY

Do not love the world nor the things in the world. If anyone loves the world, the love of the Father is not in him. For all that is in the world, the lust of the flesh and the lust of the eyes and the boastful pride of life, is not from the Father, but is from the world. The world is passing away, and also its lusts; but the one who does the will of God lives forever. 1 John 2:15-17

This is sort of a public service announcement. Through John, God is sharing wisdom. We just spoke about how He created and owns it all. He created the rules to the game. Wouldn't it benefit us to pay attention to His instruction manual?

This scripture even warns us on what to beware of: lust of the flesh (whatever feels good to the flesh, like inappropriate sexual relations, drugs, money and power, etc.), lust of the eyes (people, places and things that entice us), and boastful pride (when we feel like we've arrived and begin to look down on others or walk around puffed up on ourselves).

He is telling us DO NOT love the world, or the things in the world. Don't choose the "provision" over the "Provider." He knows we will be tempted by the things of this world.

Does this storyline sound familiar to Satan tempting Adam and Eve? What about Satan tempting Jesus?

How is Satan at work in the world today?

We have access to the world but need God's guidance. He warns us not to fall into temptation. In the world, you will find lust of the flesh, lust of the eyes and boastful pride, but that is NOT from God.

Greed, self-indulgent behavior overtakes us at times, but when we exercise discipline and wait, we sometimes allow that desire to subside.

What are some consequences for acting on impulse?

Ever want something really bad, but found out later how bad it was for you?

One of the richest and wisest men who ever lived, King Solomon had written over 3,000 proverbs used in the Bible and 1,000 songs (one of which is the book called Song of Songs). We can learn quite a bit about wealth from the man that was chosen to build God's temple in Jerusalem. Much of his time as king was characterized by his wisdom and respect for God.

Note: A good exercise is to read one book of proverbs each day of the month.

Why was Solomon blessed with so much wisdom and wealth? (*1 Kings 3:5-14*)

Can wealth be considered a byproduct of wisdom?

What does Solomon say about wealth?

We will learn throughout the study how the wisest and wealthiest man in the Bible regarded money.

Proverbs Breakdown:
A. **1:1-9:18** Wisdom for Young People
B. **10:1-24:34** Wisdom for All People
C. **25:1-31:31** Wisdom for Leaders
Solomon wrote all but four chapters in Proverbs.
Lemuel and Agur wrote chapters 22,23,24, and 31.

> *Do not wear yourself out to get rich; do not trust your own cleverness. Cast but a glance at riches, and they are gone, for they will surely sprout wings and fly off to the sky like an eagle. Proverbs 23:4-5*

It's not uncommon to hear the richest and most savvy business-men share how they've lost fortunes. We also hear of people who run through large sums of money (lottery, inheritance) due to ignorance or lack of wisdom. There is a saying, "easy come, easy go." Regardless of who you are, wealth must be accompanied by wisdom as well as humbleness.

> *He who trusts in his riches will fall, but the righteous shall flourish as the green leaf. Proverbs 11:28*

There is a feeling of security that comes with money (having the best foods, the best protection, the best healthcare, the finest clothing, jewelry, toys, etc.) but there is always the possibility of losing it.

Is it possible to have more stress with money than without it?

> *Wealth is worthless in the day of wrath, but righteousness delivers from death. Proverbs 11:4*

We know that death is separation from God. We also know God warns us: our evil and selfish desires that drive and motivate us will only draw us away from Him.

Although we may run to Him, are we prepared to relinquish our purchasing power?

Are we willing to sacrifice our immediate wants for a better and longer quality of life with God?

We cannot take a penny with us. Not one dollar we have can be used to buy us into heaven.

What are some things that money can't buy?

Love, truth, time, peace, talent, health. Money can buy the house, but it can't buy a home. Money can't buy anyone tomorrow.

> *...but the worries of this life, the deceitfulness of wealth and the desires for other things come in and choke the word, making it unfruitful. Mark 4:19*

We cannot hear God clearly when our desire is so strong that we conveniently ignore the Holy Spirit's direction. Worries- deceitfulness of wealth- desires for other things override what God has revealed to us in the Word.

Psalm 49 talks about the uncertainty of riches. A wise man is a righteous man, but a man with riches without understanding is like the beasts that perish.

> *For all can see that the wise die, that the foolish and the senseless also perish, leaving their wealth to others. Their tombs will remain their houses forever, their dwellings for endless generations, though they had named lands after themselves. People, despite their wealth, do not endure; they are like the beasts that perish. Psalms 49:10-12*

> *The Pharisees, who loved money, heard all this and were sneering at Jesus. He said to them, "You are the ones who justify yourselves in the eyes of others, but God knows your hearts. What people value highly is detestable in God's sight." Luke 16:14*

Jesus was not talking to some random men, but religious leaders. We will cover Luke 16:10-13 later on, but in paraphrase, Jesus is saying, if you can't be trusted with little, how can you be trusted with much? If you can't handle worldly wealth, how can you be trusted with true riches? If you can't manage someone else's property, who will trust you with your own property? No servant can serve two masters, etc.

The Pharisee's considered their wealth to be a sign of God's approval.

How many of us pre-judge others, looking at their wealth and immediately give them credibility?

God hates anything that will draw us away from Him. God is jealous and wants no substitute in His place.

Money can be used as a gauge by God to determine our level. He knows when we are ready to serve Him and not succumb to the temptations of worldly things that money and power produce.

> *Men prepare a meal for enjoyment, and wine makes life merry, and money is the answer to everything. Ecclesiastes 10:19*

In the last few chapters of Ecclesiastes Solomon, it concludes that it's better to have wisdom than folly. In this world, including the church, we start to believe that money is the answer to every problem, but as the satisfaction from the meal wears off, as the buzz from the wine is only temporary, the effects of our purchases soon fade away and we need/want more. Money is necessary for survival, but it warns against the love of money as it is not the Source. God alone is the provider and his provision can never replace that. We get ourselves in trouble when we start to look at money as our solution instead of God.

Key Takeaways:

1. The God who created all things warns us to not love the world or things in the world.

2. Indicators that we may be drifting away from God and into the world is the lust of the flesh, lust of the eyes, and boastful pride.

3. King Solomon tells us throughout his proverbs
to seek wisdom over wealth.

4. Wealth is deceitful. Here today and gone tomorrow if we are not
careful. Regardless of what you accumulate, it will be left behind.

5. What is highly valued among men is
detestable in God's sight. Be careful.

3. OBSESSION AND GREED

Come now, you rich, weep and howl for your miseries which are coming upon you. Your riches have rotted and your garments have become moth-eaten. Your gold and your silver have rusted; and their rust will be a witness against you and will consume your flesh like fire. It is in the last days that you have stored up your treasure! Behold, the pay of the laborers who mowed your fields, and which has been withheld by you, cries out against you; and the outcry of those who did the harvesting has reached the ears of the Lord of Sabaoth (Hosts). You have lived luxuriously on the earth and led a life of wanton (self-indulgence) pleasure; you have fattened your hearts in a day of slaughter. You have condemned and put to death the righteous man; he does not resist you. James 5:1-6

W hat do you feel drives our appetite of money to the point of obsession and greed?

Whoever loves money never has enough; whoever loves wealth is never satisfied with their income. This too is meaningless. As goods increase, so do those who consume them. And what benefit are they to the owners except to feast their eyes on them? Ecclesiastes 5:10

One of the main reasons we can't allow the lust of money to dictate our lives is because it's a never-ending chase. The lust of the flesh, the power associated with money can drive you deeper and further away from God.

A man with an evil eye hastens after wealth and does not know that want will come upon him. Proverbs 28:22

This is similar to the stingy man eager to get rich but is unaware that poverty awaits him. By hastening we are quick to do something, moving in a hurry. There is no thought behind it. It's impulsive. With money, we are often caught off guard. This is why we must seek the Holy Spirit's counsel, even in the smallest purchase. Keep in mind who the money belongs to. Keep in mind we are not owner but simply a manager of His resources. Ask God for direction. The more we are able to trust Him, the more He is able to trust us, and we break the stronghold of obsession and greed.

What good is it for a man to gain the whole world, yet forfeit his soul? Mark 8:36

Do you consider a decision to pursue more money, power, and fame a compromise on your soul?

Why does this verse seem to give an ultimatum?

What is this scripture challenging us to think about?

In this world we are inundated with advertisements and we are heavily influenced by images that drive us to seek sinful pleasure and self- indulgence. In this section of Mark, Jesus begins to predict his demise. He says to those in attendance, including the disciples, if you want to come after me, you must deny yourself, take up your cross, and follow me. Whoever loses their life for the gospel will save it.

What good is it to have all the riches, power, and fame, but spend eternity separated from God?

What we have on earth is temporary and cannot be exchanged for your soul. I never saw a U-Haul truck follow a hearse to the cemetery.

> Then he said to them, "Beware, and be on your guard against every form of greed; for not even when one has an abundance does his life consists of his possessions." Luke 12:15

Jesus never associated the good life with having money, so be careful of what society would have us to believe. Buying products to make you happy will never be a long-term solution. Having the best of everything is not worth it, if the possessions prevent you from a relationship with God.

Do you feel your relationship with God is so strong that you would recognize when He wants you to give your possessions to someone else?

Are you able to leave all possessions behind in a moment's notice if God told you so?

Are you willing to sacrifice all of eternity for temporary pleasure?

In Corinthians, Paul states

Do you not know that the wicked will not inherit the King-dom of God? Do not be deceived, neither the sexually im-moral, idolaters, adulterers, prostitutes, homosexuals, nor thieves, nor the covetous, nor drunkards, nor revilers, nor swindlers, will inherit the kingdom of God. 1 Corinthians 6:10

We cannot invite God to rule over a portion of our lives and ignore him when it comes to our personal desires. He wants us to have the desires of our heart but not if it compromises the relationship. When lustful desires are not checked, they lead to obsession and greed.

For this you know with certainty, that no immoral or im-pure person or covetous man, who is an idolater, has an inheritance in the kingdom of Christ and God. Let no one deceive you with empty words, for because of these things the wrath of God comes upon the sons of disobedience. Ephesians 5:5-6

There are plenty of messages today that use Bible scriptures to claim anything a person could desire in this world. Be aware of the spirit behind those messages. Mis quoting God's Word also has its consequences and repercussions.

"You shall not covet your neighbor's house; you shall not covet your neighbor's wife or his male servant or his female servant or his ox or his donkey or anything that belongs to your neighbor." Exodus 20:17

When we try to keep up with the Joneses or compare ourselves to others, we rob God of the opportunity to be our Father, our Pro-vider, and our Source. We look at what another has, not knowing the cost one had to pay to receive it. It could be long hours of hard work, or it could be by lying, cheating, and deceiving. This obsession drives us to cut corners and compromise our walk with God. It's stated in the Ten Commandments, and it's still relevant today.

◆ ◆ ◆

Key Takeaways:

1. A lifestyle of self-indulgence never regards God and His Word. It draws us further away from Him.

2. The appetite for money is never satisfied. Just when we think we have enough, we want more.

3. A man who is obsessed with becoming rich needs to check his heart. What is the tradeoff to being greedy for wealth? What is it worth to gain the world and lose your soul?

4. We must be mindful and stay on guard against the temptations that surround us. We are inundated with advertisements that trigger our impulses.

5. Even in church we tend to steer God's word to claim our selfish desires.

6. Don't covet what another has. We don't know the cost they paid or will pay for it. We also rob God of the opportunity to be our Provider in His will and His timing.

4. HAVING CONTENTMENT

But godliness actually is a means of great gain when accompanied by contentment. For we have brought nothing into the world, so we cannot take anything out of it either. If we have food and covering, with these we shall be content. But those who want to get rich fall into temptation and a snare and many foolish and harmful desires which plunge men into ruin and destruction. For the love of money is a root of all sorts of evil, and some by longing for it have wandered away from the faith and pierced themselves with many griefs. 1 Timothy 6:6-10

When we realize that we came into this world with nothing and we will leave with nothing, we begin to understand the precious gift we refer to as "the present." This day, not yesterday or tomorrow, we are given the ability to live, eat, drink, be clothed, and enjoy the world our Lord has created. We are not owed anything. What we have is allowed by the Almighty. Let's remember the Source and be content.

Make sure that your character is free from the love of money, being content with what you have; for He Himself has said, "I will never desert you, nor will I ever forsake you," Hebrews 13:5

There should be an assurance of knowing that God is on our side and in our corner. We can say we trust God, but those words are easily tested in the area of finances.

How can we have a character free from the love of money?

What does it mean to be content?

A state of peaceful happiness.

We have the Holy Spirit living in us, we should be full of peace. Happiness is based on external circumstances, but joy is based on internal circumstances. It's a choice that nothing happening outside of my control will affect my feelings. Joy is knowing that you may have physical ailments but being convinced that greater is He that is in you!

> *Not that I speak from want, for I have learned to be content in whatever circumstances I am. I know how to get along with humble means, and I also know how to live in prosperity; in any and every circumstance I have learned the secret of being filled and going hungry, both of having abundance and suffering need. I can do all things through Him who strengthens me. Philippians 4:11-13*

The word teaches us to be content in every circumstance. Paul lived a life of prosperity, but also had to endure prison. He's been beaten with rods, stoned, shipwrecked, robbed, hungry, thirsty, cold and naked, etc. Through all he had to endure he knew how to be content. We sometimes walk around with a sense of entitlement, as if we're never supposed to experience challenges in our lives. We must understand that God is all-knowing, and there may be a good reason why we must live through a particular season.

This is why having a relationship with God is important. Those who are not close enough to hear instruction may feel they are cursed due to their circumstances, but that can be far from the truth. Instead we must seek the Holy Spirit's counsel, the source of all prosperity, and be willing to live through a difficult season by learning contentment.

Is God the master over your possessions?

We have cute plaques and decorations that read "as for me and my house, we shall serve the Lord." Meanwhile, in the same house the core of the family structure is broken due to the mismanagement of finances.

Are we consulting God before making a purchase, or are we motivated by keeping up with our neighbors?

Have we learned to be content with what we have, or are we tempted by stuff?

> *"Do not take money from anyone by force, or accuse any-one falsely and be content with your wages." Luke 3:14*

John's message in this verse is directed to the crowds coming to be baptized by him. Among them were Roman soldiers, who were used to extorting money from people. He told them to not continue this behavior, and to learn to be content with their wages.

If you're in a job where you feel under-compensated, that is not justification to steal. We enter into a contract for our wages when we are hired. If we need more money, then we should go about it the right way, not unscrupulously.

> *"If they hear and serve Him, they will end their days in prosperity and their years in pleasures. Job 36:11*

Job lost everything but it didn't affect his relationship with God. He knew how to be content without.

How would you react to God if you suddenly lost it all?

Do you think God wants to see us prosper financially?

Do you think He asks us to be content to keep us humbled and poor?

> *Psalm 35:27- Let them shout for joy and rejoice, who favor my vindication; and let them say continually, "The Lord be magnified, who delights in the prosperity of His servant."*

Prosperity in the Bible means the peace and the welfare of God's servants. God desires David's present troubles to cease, so that he may enjoy a time of rest and tranquility. This may not mean to have more "stuff" which in and of itself does not bring fulfillment, but more important, an internal rest and contentment in the midst of trouble.

As a parent, does spoiling your children allow them to mature, or do you think just giving them "stuff" without proper advisement may set them back?

How do you feel about a balance of discipline and reward?

In *Deuteronomy 30:15-16* it says,

> "See, I have set before you today life and prosperity, and death and adversity; in that I command you today to love the Lord your God, to walk in His ways and to keep His commandments and His statutes and His judgments, that you may live and multiply, and that the Lord your God may bless you in the land where you are entering to possess it.

I don't think God wants to withhold any good thing from us. First, we must understand what God considers good. We can only know this by fellowship with Him.

How many times, even after we've been given instruction, have we consciously decided not to pay attention to God?

The Israelites are commanded to love the Lord, walk in His ways and keep His commandments, statutes and judgements as they enter into the land to possess it. Although He is all-powerful, God does allow us to make choices.

In *3 John 2*, he states

> Beloved, I pray that in all respects you may prosper and be in good health, just as your soul prospers.

"Even as your soul prospers" is critical because those without a prospered soul have a poor mentality and can never accept healing, and financial peace. We should be careful to neither neglect nor indulge ourselves. We need a balance of spiritual, mental, physical health so that we are prepared for service unto God.

Joseph, an over-confident youngster with a grand vision, literally went from the "pit to the palace." He was betrayed by his brothers, yet able to persevere through extreme hardships. He was deserted by his family, accused of sexual harassment, imprisoned, and forgotten. During these trials, he was being perfected for what ultimately would become the position of power that God revealed to him. This is why we are to draw near to God in our most vulnerable times and trust the process. We must learn to be content in our current situations.

God providence means he works behind the scene, even in the most unfavorable conditions. He says our power is perfected (matured) in weakness. He says His grace is sufficient for us. Knowing this we should be content regardless of the circumstances.

How much is enough for you?

Have you ever thought about how much you need for you and your family to live a comfortable life?

When you reach that amount, then what?

Would you be disciplined enough to give when/if God asked, or would you be obsessed with having more?

> *Jesus said to him, "If you wish to be complete, go and sell your possessions and give to the poor, and you will have treasure in heaven; and come, follow Me." But when the young man heard this statement, he went away grieving; for he was one who owned much property. And Jesus said to His disciples, "Truly I say to you, it is hard for a rich man to enter the kingdom of heaven. Again, I say to you, it is easier for a camel to go through the eye of a needle, than for a rich man to enter the kingdom of God." When the disciples heard this, they were very astonished and said,*

"Then who can be saved?" And looking at them Jesus said to them, "With people this is impossible, but with God all things are possible." Matthew 19:21-26

Key Takeaways:

1. Godliness is accompanied by contentment.

2. Being free from the love of money allows God to work in and around us. Our assurance in our Source allows us to be content.

3. God gives us strength to have contentment in all circumstances. In fact, He takes pleasure in the prosperity (peace) of His people.

4. Being content for some is seen as failure, or a sign of submission. For God, it displays one's strength and exposes another's weakness. How we respond to humbling circumstances tells us a lot about our character.

5. Be careful not to neglect or indulge ourselves. We need a balance of spiritual, mental, and physical health.

6. How much do you need to be content? What amount of income and savings would it take? When you attain that amount, then what?

B. THE GOOD STEWARD OF MONEY

5. WORKING FOR MONEY

The Lord God took the man and put him in the garden of Eden to work it and keep it. Genesis 2:15

When God placed Adam in the garden, he gave him a "job." A responsibility of working the land, cultivating, and watching it produce. This was an awesome duty delegated to man, proving how our heavenly Father esteems man. God did not give this responsibility to angels but to human (spirits made in the image of God, within a body made up of dirt). We're each given the ability to put God's image on display as the Adam of our personal Garden of Eden.

Working is a not only something God ordained, but it should be considered a privilege. We are called by God to serve our fellow man in some capacity. God expects a return on the talents, gifts and skills we are blessed with.

Do you believe working is something we must do as Christians?

Do you think working conflicts with God being our Provider?

Are there any spiritual traits or characteristics associated with working?

> But if anyone does not provide for his relatives, and espe-
> cially for members of his household, he has denied the faith
> and is worse than an unbeliever. 1 Timothy 5:8

Family relationships are important in God's eyes. As parents, especially fathers, we have a responsibility to take care of our children and immediate family members. Even adult children and
grandchildren have a responsibility to care for the elders (parents/
grandparents) in the event they have no one to help them.

> But if a widow has children or grandchildren, let them first
> learn to show godliness to their own household and to make
> some return to their parents, for this is pleasing in the sight
> of God. 1 Timothy 5:4

> Whatever you do, work heartily, as for the Lord and not for
> men. Colossians 3:23

When we are engaged in the covenant relationship between ourselves and the Father, we realize it's His job to provide for our
needs.

Why is it so important that we work, and work heartily, and most
important as unto the Lord?

How we respond to work is taken into spiritual consideration. Nothing we do is in the closet with God. Regardless of our employer, co-workers, or employees, we answer to a higher calling, and how we treat others ultimately reflects back on us.

For you yourselves know how you ought to imitate us, because we were not idle when we were with you, nor did we eat anyone's bread without paying for it, but with toil and labor we worked night and day, that we might not be a burden to any of you. It was not because we do not have that right, but to give you in ourselves an example to imitate. 2 Thessalonians 3:7-9

This is Paul's warning against idleness. Paul and his team were in Thessalonica doing ministry work, and would have been justified, but they wanted to show they were not lazy. They were an example to the people about having a good work ethic. When we don't work, someone else must carry the weight. We put others in a position to work harder. Paul also recognized one's work ethic has spiritual principles. He goes on to say,

for even when we were with you, we would give you this command: If anyone is not willing to work, let him not eat. 2 Thessalonians 3:10

Resting is important. There is also time for leisure or recreation, but there is also a time to work. This scripture should not be taken out of context in referring to those who are unable to work, but it also should not be used as an excuse.

Now such persons we command and encourage in the Lord Jesus Christ to do their work quietly and to earn their own living. 2 Thessalonians 3:12

We must ask ourselves, if we are not working, then what are we doing with that time?

How many justifications do you think we really have for avoiding work?

As a provider, do you think God uses our skills to earn us a certain amount of money?

Can that money earned be used to live a comfortable lifestyle?

Through our work God is able to bless other areas of our lives. Some of the things we desire that God approves can be purchased because we have the means to afford them by earning a living.

> And to aspire to live quietly, and to mind your own affairs, and to work with your hands, as we instructed you, so that you may walk properly before outsiders and be dependent on no one. 1 Thessalonians 4:11-12

The Thessalonians were so excited about Jesus' return that some of them quit their jobs. You cannot be a good witness for Christ if you are seen as lazy, and always looking for a hand-out from others.

The scripture says to mind your own affairs and to work with your hands. We should be seen more than we are heard by outsiders.

What kind of representation of God would we be if we're seen as lazy?

What would that do to our testimony?

All it takes is one bad day to ruin your reputation. We must ask

God to work through us so that we reflect a hard-working, godly image.

How do you think a good reputation translates in other areas of life?

> *Do you see a man skillful in his work? He will stand before kings; he will not stand before obscure men. Proverbs 22:29*

As representation of Christ, we should not only have a standard of excellence, but not be surprised when God wants to put our skills and talents on display. God is proud of us when we do our work unto Him.

What about the person who works hard, and is never recognized, never rewarded, or even acknowledged?

What about the person who does all the work just for someone else to receive the promotion or accolades?

> *Let the thief no longer steal, but rather let him labor, doing honest work with his own hands, so that he may have some-thing to share with anyone in need. Ephesians 4:28*

Not only are we to work, but to make an honest living by doing right by our bosses and customers by not ripping anyone off.

> *And because he was of the same trade he stayed with them and worked, for they were tentmakers by trade. Acts 18:3*

It was customary for Jewish boys to learn a trade. For Paul and Aquila (and Priscilla) it was tent-making. The tents made of goat's skin were used to house soldiers. Because of their trade, they were able to make a living by selling tents to the Roman army. With this sort of skill, Paul could make a living anywhere. God blesses us with the gifts and talents that we need to support our livelihood.

They ended up partnering together in ministry by a common trade of tent-making.

How many people have we met through work that God has orchestrated for His glory?

By the way, tent-making was not their primary job. God was able to use their trade of tent-making to finance their ministry, their primary job.

When we allow God to be in control, he is able to choreograph moves that aren't logical. God may have a career change in store for you at some point, but we must be in tune to hear the direction. Nevertheless, it is highly unlikely that God is calling you away from work, without a job to replace it. He gets more glory from us in the marketplace than at home.

How many hours in a day do we spend at work?

Is there opportunity for you to be used by God in the workplace?

If we are willing, I'm sure opportunities would present themselves.

Quite often we are impatient when it comes to our jobs/careers. We want to climb the corporate ladder over-night, but God wants us to learn as we mature and prepare for a higher position.

How many times have we heard of the entry-level underdog that ends up running the company some day?

In **Zechariah 4:10**, it says

> *do not despise these small beginnings, for the LORD rejoices to see the work begin.*

There is honor in paying dues while on the job.

What does Proverbs have to say regarding our attitude toward working?

> *Poor is he who works with a negligent hand, but the hand of the diligent makes rich. Proverbs 10:4*

> *The sluggard does not plow in the autumn; he will seek at harvest and have nothing. Proverbs 20:4*

> *Whoever is slack in his work is a brother to him who destroys. Proverbs 18:9*

> *I passed by the field of a sluggard, by the vineyard of a man lacking sense, and behold, it was all overgrown with thorns; the ground was covered with nettles, and its stone wall was broken down. Then I saw and considered it; I looked and received instruction. A little sleep, a little slumber, a little folding of the hands to rest, and poverty will come upon you like a robber, and want like an armed man. Proverbs 24:30-34*

Love not sleep, lest you come to poverty; open your eyes, and you will have plenty of bread. Proverbs 20:13

In all toil there is profit, but mere talk tends only to poverty. Proverbs 14:23

He who tills his land will have plenty of bread, but he who pursues worthless things lacks sense. Proverbs 12:11

A lazy man does not roast his prey, but the precious possession of a man is diligence. Proverbs 12:27

What does the Word say about women and work?

Titus 2:4-5 states

Then they can urge the younger women to love their husbands and children, to be self-controlled and pure, to be busy at home, to be kind, and to be subject to their husbands, so that no one will malign the word of God.

As the wife submits to her husband, there may be a need to first take care of the home before looking outside for work. In today's world, two incomes are beneficial and even necessary. This is not to discourage a woman from working or simply to keep her at home, but there is an order for man to provide and a woman to support the household.

What sort of order is implemented in your household?

I must expound, that men and women are of equal value in the sight of God. Both created in His image. However, in God's grand order, there's a need for a particular structure, making the man the head of the household. For example, God the Father, the Son, and the Holy Spirit are all equal, but each play a prominent role depending on the circumstance. Even if the woman earns more money, the man should still be the head of the household.

If the wife works a full-time job as the man, what are the expectations once everyone returns home? Who is responsible for what?

It could be recommended that in early child years the wife stays home more, but during the child's older years there is more freedom to explore employment opportunities, if necessary. Married couples should pray about this. Weigh out the value of work vs the value of helping the home at home.

If a man has the heart to serve the Lord and provide for His family, I believe that God will have no choice but to honor that man and that marriage. As our hearts are willing, God is faithful.

Proverbs 31:10-27 talks about the woman of noble character, who prioritizes her home. The husband is blessed by her. She brings more than just beauty or riches. She personifies the balanced life for a mother/wife. She is more "for the home" than she is "in the home."

What does the Word say about having business partners?

There are scriptures about being unequally yoked

2 Corinthians 6:14-18, for what partnership has right-eousness with lawlessness?

The scripture discourages partnerships with non-believers. Even with Christians, the scripture says to be careful.

◆ ◆ ◆

Key Takeaways:

1. Man was created to work.

2. It is a privilege to work unto God.

3. We have an obligation to take care of our family, especially our immediate family. This goes for parents taking care of their children, as well as adult children taking care of their parents.

4. A man who does not work does not deserve to eat.

5. God uses our skills to produce an income for our livelihood.

6. A man skillful in his work stands among kings. God's glory is displayed when we put our hearts into our assignment.

7. Paul used his trade as a tentmaker to support himself as he traveled in ministry.

8. Don't despise small beginnings.

9. Men and women are seen as equal in God's sight. However, the man is the head of the household. A woman's submission should not be seen as her being inferior

to her husband, but in support of her husband.

6. DISHONEST MONEY

then it shall be, when he sins and becomes guilty, that he shall restore what he took by robbery or what he got by extortion, or the deposit which was entrusted to him or the lost thing which he found, or anything about which he swore falsely; he shall make restitution for it in full and add to it one-fifth more. He shall give it to the one to whom it belongs on the day he presents his guilt offering. Leviticus 6:4-5

According to CNBC, workplace theft is costing US businesses around $50B per year in 2016. That's close to $1B per week!

What are some examples of workplace theft?

From paperclips and pencils to coming in late or leaving early, it all adds up. If we are doing our work as unto the Lord, we are mindful of how our actions affect our employers. We are able to display integrity in the smallest most insignificant areas.

Would you pass the test if your boss went undercover? Would you be promoted, or fired?

Outside of work, are there other ways that we "steal" from others?

What about hotel amenities, magazines at doctor's offices, taking extra straws, napkins and condiments from a fast-food restaurant?

What do the Proverbs have to say about dishonest gain?

> *Wealth obtained by fraud dwindles, but the one who gathers by labor increases it. Proverbs 13:11*

> *He who oppresses the poor to make more for himself or who gives to the rich, will only come to poverty. Proverbs 22:16*

> *A good name is to be chosen rather than great riches, loving favor rather than silver and gold. Proverbs 22:1*

> *He who increases his wealth by interest and usury gathers it for him who is gracious to the poor. Proverbs 28:8*

> *Great wealth is in the house of the righteous, but trouble is in the income of the wicked. Proverbs 15:6*

> *He who profits illicitly troubles his own house, but he who hates bribes will live. Proverbs 15:27*

The acquisition of treasures by a lying tongue Is a fleeting vapor, the pursuit of death. Proverbs 21:6

Differing weights are an abomination to the Lord, and a false scale is not good Proverbs 20:23

The greatest command in the scripture is followed by the second greatest command in the scripture:

and you shall love the Lord your God with all your heart, and with all your soul, and with all your mind, and with all your strength.' The second is this, 'You shall love your neighbor as yourself.' There is no other commandment greater than these." Mark 12:31

The vertical love of God and the horizontal love of our neighbor is the sum total of all God's commands. As we bring money under this microscope, it becomes apparent that we fall short in many subtle areas regarding dishonest scales. We should be challenged by this to consider what we do on a daily basis, not taking even the small things for granted.

How can we expect to be trusted with God's resources if we don't consider our neighbors?

Have you ever wondered why the wicked prosper?

Read Jeremiah 12. It is known as Jeremiah's Prayer (or complaint), where he asks God about the prosperity of the wicked. He doesn't understand why God allows this to happen. God does not give him the answer he expected, but instead challenges Jeremiah to look at self.

Righteous are You, O Lord, that I would plead my case with You; Indeed, I would discuss matters of justice with You: Why has the way of the wicked prospered? Why are all those who deal in treachery at ease? You have planted them, they have also taken root; They grow, they have even produced fruit. You are near to their lips but far from their mind. But You know me, O Lord; You see me; And You examine my heart's attitude toward You. Drag them off like sheep for the slaughter and set them apart for a day of carnage! How long is the land to mourn and the vegetation of the countryside to wither? For the wickedness of those who dwell in it,

Animals and birds have been snatched away, because men have said, "He will not see our latter ending. If you have run with footmen and they have tired you out, then how can you compete with horses? If you fall down in a land of peace, How will you do in the thicket of the Jordan? "For even your brothers and the household of your father, even they have dealt treacherously with you, even they have cried aloud after you. Do not believe them, although they may say nice things to you."

God's Answer:

"I have forsaken My house, I have abandoned My inheritance; I have given the beloved of My Soul Into the hand of her enemies. "My inheritance has become to Me Like a lion in the forest; She has roared against Me; Therefore, I have come to hate her. "Is My inheritance like a speckled bird of prey to Me? Are the birds of prey against her on every side? Go, gather all the beasts of the field, bring them to devour! "Many shepherds have ruined My vineyard, they

have trampled down My field; They have made My pleasant field A desolate wilderness. "It has been made a desolation, Desolate, it mourns before Me; The whole land has been made desolate, because no man lays it to heart. "On all the bare heights in the wilderness Destroyers have come, for a sword of the Lord is devouring from one end of the land even to the other;

There is no peace for anyone. "They have sown wheat and have reaped thorns, they have strained themselves to no profit. But be ashamed of you harvest Because of the fierce anger of the Lord."Thus, says the Lord concerning all My wicked neighbors who strike at the inheritance with which I have endowed My people Israel, Behold I am about to uproot them from their land and will uproot the house of Judah from among them. And it will come about that after I have uprooted them, I will again have compassion on them; and I will bring them back, each one to his inheritance and each one to his land. Then if they will really learn the ways of My people, to swear by My name, 'As the Lord lives,' even as they taught My people to swear by Baal, they will be built up in the midst of My people. But if they will not listen, then I will uproot that nation, uproot and destroy it," declares the Lord.

God's word is simple and direct- obey, and be blessed, or disobey, and be cursed. Today, we have two commands from God, to love Him with all of our heart, and to love our neighbor. God did not explain, nor does he need to justify what He allows to happen. Instead, we must learn to not look outside of ourselves, or be envious of others. There is no excuse for being dishonest with money.

Would you rather do what God commands, even if it doesn't pay an earthly dividend, or would you rather live like the wicked, and prosper here and now?

Psalm 73 talks about the contrast of the wicked and the righteous.

Surely God is good to Israel, to those who are pure in heart! But as for me, my feet came close to stumbling, my steps had almost slipped. For I was envious of the arrogant As I saw the prosperity of the wicked. For there are no pains in their death,
And their body is fat. They are not in trouble as other men, nor are they plagued like mankind. Therefore, pride is their necklace; The garment of violence covers them. Their eye bulges from fatness;
The imaginations of their heart run riot. They mock and wickedly speak of oppression; They speak from on high. They have set their mouth against the heavens, And their tongue parades through the earth. Therefore, his people return to this place, and waters of abundance are drunk by them. They say, "How does God know?
And is there knowledge with the Most-High?" Behold, these are the wicked; And always at ease, they have increased in wealth. Surely in vain I have kept my heart pure and washed my hands in innocence;
For I have been stricken all day long and chastened every morning.

If I had said, "I will speak thus," Behold, I would have betrayed the generation of Your children. When I pondered to understand this, it was troublesome in my sight Until I came into the sanctuary of God; Then I perceived their end. Surely You set them in slippery places; You cast them down to destruction. How they are destroyed in a moment! They are utterly swept away by sudden terrors! Like a dream when one awakes, O Lord, when aroused, you will despise their form. When my heart was embittered and I was pier-

ced within, Then I was senseless and ignorant; I was like a beast before You. Nevertheless, I am continually with You; You have taken hold of my right hand. With Your Counsel You will guide me, and afterward receive me to glory. Whom have I in heaven but You? And besides You, I desire nothing on earth. My flesh and my heart may fail, But God is the strength of my heart and my portion forever. For, behold, those who are far from You will perish; You have destroyed all those who are unfaithful to You. But as for me, the nearness of God is my good; I have made the Lord God my refuge, that I may tell of all Your works.

We are deceived by the wealth of the wicked, but we have nothing to despise because in the end, God's way is the best way. When we get caught up in the world and into the glamour and riches, just think! God can make you rich, but He can also give salvation which is better than being wealthy. Don't be deceived, it's all smoke and mirrors set up by Satan. To follow the world's ways just to get paid is a foolish and deadly move.

> *The Lord's Prayer reads "And forgive us our debts, as we also have forgiven our debtors." Matthew 6:12*

This has to do with forgiving others. As we are forgiven for our sin, we are to forgive others against us. God is sovereign and takes negative circumstances to work out for our good.

Draw closer to God when you feel being good is not benefiting you. He will reveal what being bad can do!

◆ ◆ ◆

Key Takeaways:

1. There are penalties for being dishonest with money.

2. Proverbs tell us explicitly that wealth obtained dishonestly dwindles away. Those who oppress the poor bring it on themselves. A good name is better than riches. Those who profit illicitly trouble their own house.

3. In many subtle and unintentional ways, we may be stealing, so before you look at someone else's issues, check yourself.

4. If we need a moral compass, run all of our decisions through God's commandment to first love Him with all of our heart, soul, mind, and strength, and then to love our neighbor as ourselves. If we do this, we will not have an issue.

5. Never despise the rich, God's way is always better.

7. LIVING IN DEBT

Owe nothing to anyone except to love one another; for he who loves his neighbor has fulfilled the law. Romans 13:8

According to Lexington Law, the average consumer debt in the US is around $11,000 (credit card debt) 2018. Statistics say that those who pay with a credit card tend to spend 1/3 more than those who use cash.

Reports indicate that Americans have been amassing more and more debt since 2013. We are losing our financial literacy at an alarming rate. Auto loans totaled over $1T in 2018. This suggests that 70% of automobiles in U.S. are financed. The average student loan/total students enrolled in public/private universities in 2018 is $76,468. Student loans now total around $1.5T.

According to Howard Dayton of Crown Financial Ministries, 50% of those who perform "plastic surgery" on their credit cards actually follow through and become debt free. He also suggests if you can't pay it by the end of the month, you should not have it.

Debt is a form of slavery that strips a man of his peace of mind. It's often a substitute for hard work. It undermines God's ability to provide for us in His way and in His timing. Debt is used to override what we know in our heart is not God's will. It proves our lack of trust in God. It takes away our ability to provide and/or be generous (when we are indebted to another). We are unable to get proper rest when we have to work two jobs and a side hustle to pay off debt.

> "She came and told the man of God, and he said, 'Go, sell the oil and pay your debts, and you and your sons can live on the rest.'" 2 Kings 4:7

In this verse, this widow's husband had owed money and the creditor was coming to take her two boys as slaves. Notice the affect that debt has on our family, even in our absence. This particular creditor was not a very understanding person. Although Christians live by a standard, we cannot assume our creditors will be lenient when we owe them. God was able to perform miracles through Elisha on this woman's behalf, but this does not give us a pass to be financially irresponsible, expecting God to come in and save us.

> There were also those who said, 'We are mortgaging our fields, our vineyards, and our houses to get grain because of the famine.' And there were those who said, "We have borrowed money for the king's tax on our fields and our vineyards. Now our flesh is as the flesh of our brothers, our children are as their children. Yet we are forcing our sons and our daughters to be slaves, and some of our daughters have already been enslaved, but it is not in our power to help it, for other men have our fields and our vineyards." Nehemiah 5:3-5

During this time, rich countrymen would lend large sums of money to the Jews, then when a payment was missed, they would take over their fields. Without income, they were forced to sell their children into slavery.

Could you imagine the consequences of your debt being to sell your own kids into slavery? How would you react?

> *"They lay themselves down beside every altar on garments taken in pledge, and in the house of their God they drink the wine of those who have been fined." Amos 2:8*

When Israel turned away from God, they found themselves in trouble. As a result, they lived in lack and were indebted to others.

> *The rich rules over the poor, and the borrower is the slave of the lender. Proverbs 22:7*

Is there ever a reason to not pay what you owe?

What if you've dug yourself so far in a hole that you cannot see your way out?

What about paying taxes?

The scripture is clear that we are never to give our hearts to our government, but we are to obey the law and pay taxes to those we owe taxes and pay honor to those we owe honor.

> *"Pay to all what is owed to them: taxes to whom taxes are owed, revenue to whom revenue is owed, respect to whom respect is owed, honor to whom honor is owed." Romans 13:7*

> *"If you lend money to any of my people with you who is poor, you shall not be like a moneylender to him, and you shall not exact interest from him. If ever you take your*

neighbor's cloak in pledge, you shall return it to him before the sun goes down, for that is his only covering, and it is his cloak for his body; in what else shall he sleep? And if he cries to me, I will hear, for I am compassionate." Exodus 22:25-27

God saw it as bad for one to hold a debt over another's head and deprive them of their basic needs because of a debt. This is why He doesn't want us to put ourselves in a position of owing someone else. One who has should not use another's basic needs as collateral in pledge.

Do you lend money to others? If so, what is your criteria?

"And this is the manner of the release: every creditor shall release what he has lent to his neighbor. He shall not exact it of his neighbor, his brother, because the Lord's release has been proclaimed." Deuteronomy 15:2

Though a creditor could collect from a foreigner, during the seventh year or Sabbath year, the debts of fellow Israelites were cancelled. This was God's original plan during that time.

How do you think this would work out for us today?

Because of the consequences of debt, God prefers us to be lenders and not borrowers, because a borrower is slave to the lender.

"For the Lord your God will bless you, as he promised you, and you shall lend to many nations, but you shall not borrow, and you shall rule over many nations, but they shall not rule over you." Deuteronomy 15:6

The blessing of God does not come in the form of debt. The new car that ends up being a huge financial burden was likely not the blessing God is referring to. God wants us in a debt-free position, so we can move around freely doing His will.

What does the Bible say about co-signing?

"One who lacks sense gives a pledge and puts up security in the presence of his neighbor." Proverbs 17:18

My son, if you have become surety for your neighbor, have given a pledge for a stranger, if you have been snared with the words of your mouth, have been caught with the words of your mouth, do this then, my son, and deliver yourself; Since you have come into the hand of your neighbor, Go, humble yourself, and importune (harass) your neighbor. Give no sleep to your eyes, nor slumber to your eyelids; Deliver yourself like a gazelle from the hunter's hand and like a bird from the hand of the fowler. Proverbs 6:1-5

Solomon warns his son not to put up security for his neighbor. Don't involve yourself into another person's financial arrangement. Don't rest until you've run fast and far from this situation. Do not be someone's co-signer!

"Be not one of those who give pledges, who put up security for debts. If you have nothing with which to pay, why should your bed be taken from under you?" Proverbs 22:26-27

Chances are, if you can't pay it by the end of the month, you should not have it.

We relinquish our freedom to spend, when we are legally obligated to repay. Compound interest is a powerful model, regardless of which side of it you are on. Living beyond our means is basically telling God that we want now, regardless of the consequences. It also says we have the wisdom to handle our own financial situation. Without an ability to buy now, we borrow to pay later. This is not God's will.

How should we approach financing a house or a car?

Must we first have every penny before we make a purchase?

Ideally, yes, but there is a difference between owing on something you will eventually own and can potentially increase in value, and something that doesn't have value or will depreciate.

Am I purchasing an asset or a liability?

Borrowing to purchase a home or car that we cannot truly afford is a burden, not a blessing.

Cars depreciate in value, but there is value in getting you to the workplace, where you earn money.

Does this mean to buy a $50,000 car on a $25,000 salary?

Does the value of your purchase equal or exceed the loan payment, or are you paying $30,000 over the course of the loan for a car that is only worth $15,000 if you sold it today?

What is a good percentage to use as a rule of thumb for the purchase of a home and a car?

It is suggested not to exceed 28% of your gross monthly income when paying your mortgage (Rule of 28). Put another way, your house should not cost more than 2.5 years of salary. Lenders will likely extend you up to 4-5 times your salary. Car buyers should spend no more than 10% of their take home pay on a car loan payment, and no more than 20% on car expenses.

The Word also warns us about presuming that we'll have the money to pay tomorrow.

> Come now, you who say, "Today or tomorrow we will go to such and such a city, and spend a year there and engage in business and make a profit." James 4:13

God does not like pride and arrogance. Although it's wise to make plans for the future. We shouldn't be arrogant to think that tomorrow is a guarantee.

If this is correct, how can we make a purchase today and be so confident in knowing that it will be paid back in the future?

Let's not deny God the ability to provide His way and in His time. There are lessons we can learn from patience.

God also expects us to be men of integrity if we are in a debt.

> "If a man borrows anything of his neighbor, and it is injured or dies, the owner not being with it, he shall make full restitution." Exodus 22:14

> Do not withhold good from those to whom it is due, when it is in your power to do it. Do not say to your neighbor, "Go, and come back, and tomorrow I will give it," When you have it with you. Proverbs 3:27-28

If you've borrowed, and you have the means to pay today, don't put it off until tomorrow.

Is it right to go on vacation, knowing you owe your neighbor?

> *The wicked borrows and does not pay back, but the righteous is gracious and gives. Psalm 37:21*

In conclusion, let us look toward our Lord and Savior, Jesus Christ. Regardless of our financial standing, we were all on a path of destruction due to the wages of sin. Financial debt also has spiritual implications as there are consequences for not paying the cost. Our sins cost more than we can afford, but our debt has been paid-in-full.

> *"By canceling the record of debt that stood against us with its legal demands. This he set aside, nailing it to the cross." Colossians 2:14*

We're granted freedom through Christ, and an opportunity to live the life God has promised for us on earth, if we seek first the Kingdom of God. Let us not run back and become slaves to the system that is meant to oppress us.

Key Takeaways:

1. Consumer debt continues to grow, proving that as a nation we've not sought godly counsel regarding our purchases.

2. A debt back in the day could result in you or your children being sold in slavery. One who is unable to

pay debt literally became a slave to the lender.

3. As believers, we should not hold debt over someone's head and deprive them of their basic living needs. At the same time, we cannot expect our creditors to be as understanding.

4. God's will for us is to be lenders, not borrowers, because debt limits our mobility and stifles our growth. We're stripped of rest when we work two jobs and a side hustle to pay off a debt.

5. Pay taxes and honor to those owed (in government) but do not give them your heart.

6. Do not cosign for another, run fast and far from anyone who asks.

7. When buying a home, use the Rule of 28, or no more than 28% of your gross monthly income. When buying a car, do not exceed 10% of your monthly income.

8. If you borrow from your neighbor, don't rest until you have paid it back. Even if he dies, make full restitution. Only the wicked borrows and doesn't pay back.

9. Jesus paid the ultimate price for our debt (of sin) in His death. Do not allow His death to be in vain by becoming a slave to someone over finances.

8. MONEY MANAGEMENT

"He who is faithful in a very little thing is faithful also in much; and he who is unrighteous in a very little thing is unrighteous also in much. Therefore, if you have not been faithful in the use of unrighteous wealth, who will entrust the true riches to you? And if you have not been faithful in the use of that which is another's, who will give you that which is your own? Luke 16:10-12

What is a steward?

One who manages another's property. To protect and expand the assets of another.

Will we ever take ownership of God's property?

Until we comprehend the truth that God is the owner of all, and we are simply stewards, we'll never be in a position for God to trust us with more.

Money management has spiritual significance. The power and meaning we give to our money reveal how we manage our lives. This is why the topic of money is discussed so much in the bible. If we're faithful to Him in every area of our lives including with our substance (finances, possessions, etc.), we can be entrusted with more.

> *Wealth gained hastily will dwindle, but whoever gathers little by little will increase it. Proverbs 13:11*

Wealth is not built over night, but usually over time. It's not a get rich quick scheme, but a practical means to accomplishing a financial goal.

> *The wise store up choice food and olive oil, but fools gulp theirs down. Proverbs 21:20*

A wise person does not live in waste or spend money prodigiously (extravagant and recklessly wasteful).

> *The plans of the diligent lead to profit as surely as haste leads to poverty. Proverbs 21:5*

If we're able to pause and seek counsel with God on our purchases, we should notice how our impulsive shopping decisions only lead to future heartache.

> *Go to the ant, you sluggard; consider its ways and be wise! It has no commander, no overseer or ruler, yet it stores its provisions in summer and gathers its food at harvest. Proverbs 6:6-8*

Being lazy is never an excuse in the Kingdom of God. We must be diligent in what we do. Solomon uses ants as an example of diligent labor, and a blueprint of how to save.

The Parable of the Talents in Matthew 25:14-30 gives us a great illustration of how God views our ability to manage money. Let us investigate this parable.

> "For it is just like a man about to go on a journey, who called his own slaves and entrusted his possessions to them.

Has not God entrusted us with his possessions for us to manage for him?

> To one he gave five talents, to another, two, and to another, one, each according to his own ability; and he went on his journey.

Each was given money according to their own ability. This tells us that God will not give us more than He thinks we can handle.

> Immediately the one who had received the five talents went and traded with them, and gained five more talents. In the same manner, the one who had received the two talents gained two more. But he who received the one talent went away, and dug a hole in the ground and hid his master's money.

As we've studied previously, God expects a return on His investment in us. Regardless of the magnitude, we are each called to be stewards of God's possessions. No two people have the same amount of time, talents or treasures to work with, as Tony Evans suggests, but each will be held accountable for the portion they are entrusted to manage. Money isn't just for our enjoyment, but kingdom advancement.

> "Now after a long time the master of those slaves came and settled accounts with them. The one who had received the five talents came up and brought five more talents, saying, 'Master, you entrusted five talents to me. See, I have gained five more talents.' His master said to him, 'Well done, good and faithful slave. You were faithful with a few things, I will put you in charge of many things; enter into the joy of your master.

This scripture can be seen as figurative and literal. It's talking directly about money, but we can also relate the talent to our skills, abilities, and talents of which God has blessed us.

We are told in a couple of scriptures how one who is faithful with little will be entrusted with more. Like the man, Jesus has left us with resources to manage.

This verse also mentions that it took the master a long time to come back and settle his accounts.

What are you doing with the assets God has blessed you with?

What kind of returns are you receiving, or, are you living only for the here and now, without any regard for God or anyone else?

One day, we will all have to account for the talents (figurative and literal) that we've been given.

What is the Rule of 72?

This is a formula that is used to explain how long it would take for your money to double, according to the percentage of returns you are expecting. If you expect a 7% return on your investment, this means that every ten years your savings/investments would double. If you were given $10,000 at twenty years old, it would double four times by the time you turn sixty ($20,000, $40,000, $80,000, $160,000), for a total of $160,000.

Would you view the person who invested $10,000 for 7% returns over the next forty years a "good steward?"

Being a good steward is an offensive strategy as well as defensive strategy. If we're mindful not to incur excessive debt and to live within our means, we not only have more financial freedom and flexibility, but we put ourselves in a position to be trusted with more as the scriptures indicate.

> "Also, the one who had received the two talents came up and said, 'Master, you entrusted two talents to me. See, I have gained two more talents. His master said to him, 'Well done, good and faithful slave. You were faithful with a few things, I will put you in charge of many things; enter into the joy of your master.'

Like the one with five talents, the one with two talents were also faithful and will now be put in charge of many things. Although both were doubled, they did not receive the same blessing. We do not have to compare ourselves to the next person. God knows exactly what each person is capable of. What may not be enough for one may be more than enough for another. Nevertheless, God blessed them both according to their abilities.

> "And the one also who had received the one talent came up and said, 'Master, I knew you to be a hard man, reaping where you did not sow and gathering where you scattered

no seed. And I was afraid, and went away and hid your talent in the ground. See, you have what is yours.'

The one with one talent immediately steps up with the negative, pessimistic view. In hindsight, it's easy to criticize this slave, but let's take a look at his mindset.

How many of us view God as a big tyrant in the sky- looking over our shoulders, waiting for us to make a mistake so he can punish us? Or, do you view God as a big push over- taking his counsel for granted and using His possessions without consideration?

This slave was lazy! He didn't even want to deposit the talent in the bank. He wasn't concerned with his master's affairs. He was selfish and inconsiderate, returning to the master exactly what he received.

> *"But his master answered and said to him, 'You wicked, lazy slave, you knew that I reap where I did not sow and gather where I scattered no seed. Then you ought to have put my money in the bank, and on my arrival, I would have received my money back with interest. Therefore, take away the talent from him, and give it to the one who has the ten talents.'*

We are each called for a purpose, but if we are not willing to step up to the plate, God will get the job done elsewhere. Do we really want to be overlooked by God, or seen as a person that God cannot rely on? God doesn't expect us to be perfect, but He expects faithfulness and obedience.

One reason we are to trust and have faith is because there will be things ahead that we cannot see. As we are obedient, we are trusted with more. There is a blessing directly connected to our obedience. On the flip side of the coin, there are consequences for disobedience.

> *"For to everyone who has, more shall be given, and he will have an abundance; but from the one who does not have, even what he does have shall be taken away. Throw out the worthless slave into the outer darkness; in that place, there will be weeping and gnashing of teeth.*

As in the parable of the talents, Jesus expects us to be prepared for His return at any moment. The slave with the one talent was not prepared for his master's return.

What are we doing to be prepared for His return?

> *Peter said, "Lord, are You addressing this parable to us, or to everyone else as well?" And the Lord said, "Who then is the faithful and sensible steward, whom his master will put in charge of his servants, to give them their rations at the proper time? Blessed is that slave whom his master finds so doing when he comes. Truly I say to you that he will put him in charge of all his possessions. But if that slave says in his heart, 'My master will be a long time in coming,' and begins to beat the slaves, both men and women, and to eat and drink and get drunk; the master of that slave will come on a day when he does not expect him and at an hour he does not know, and will cut him in pieces, and assign him a place with the unbelievers. And that slave who knew his master's will and did not get ready or act in accord with his will, will receive many lashes, but the one who did not know it, and committed deeds worthy of a flogging, will receive but few. From everyone who has been given much, much will be required; and to whom they entrusted much, of him they will ask all the more. Luke 12:41-48*

This is about Christ's return, but it looks at it from a steward's perspective.

Do we have the qualities of a good steward? Are we sincere, fearless, trusting, and generous?

God wants a willing servant who will be a good steward. If you do what you are told, He will put you in charge of more, but if you don't, He will assign the task to someone else. No one knows when Christ will return, so this cannot be a ploy just to earn a reward. It must be genuine.

> *Let Pharaoh appoint commissioners over the land to take a fifth of the harvest of Egypt during the seven years of abundance. They should collect all the food of these good years that are coming and store up the grain under the authority of Pharaoh, to be kept in the cities for food. This food should be held in reserve for the country, to be used during the seven years of famine that will come upon Egypt, so that the country may not be ruined by the famine. Genesis 41:34-36*

God is using Joseph to interpret Pharaoh's dream about the cows and the grain. He did not expect, nor was he prepared for a famine. In addition to the interpretation, Joseph also had a strategy for Pharaoh to implement. Because of Pharaoh's confidence in Joseph, he put Joseph in charge of his palace.

God gave Joseph favor. With his favor that upgraded his position (from the pit to the palace) Joseph had the wisdom of God to be a good steward. He showed Pharaoh how to strategically plan out the next 14 years. The only way to prevent starvation was through careful planning. Without this plan, Egypt would have turned from prosperity to ruin. God's favor and wisdom, followed by practical implementation, will work miracles in your financial future.

> *On the first day of every week, each one of you should set aside a sum of money in keeping with your income, saving it up, so that when I come no collections will have to be made. 1 Corinthians 16:2*

It is wise to put away and save. Another great illustration of this comes from ants!

> *Four things on earth are small, yet they are extremely wise: Ants are creatures of little strength, yet they store up their food in the summer. Proverbs 30:24-25*

Saving is a simple concept, but what makes this ant so wise?

They are of little strength, yet they prepare well. They realize that what we put away today makes tomorrow that much easier.

When we understand compound interest, our savings becomes an investment vehicle and we begin to turn our money into our little workers.

Generational wealth:

> *A good person leaves an inheritance for their children's children, but a sinner's wealth is stored up for the righteous. Proverbs 13:22*

Solomon in his wisdom suggests that we not only store up for ourselves, but enough for our grandchildren. This verse also talks about kingdom economics. Although the wicked accumulate wealth, God has a way of redirecting it for His purpose.

> *For which of you, intending to build a tower, does not sit down first and count the cost, whether he has enough to finish it—lest, after he has laid the foundation, and is not able to finish, all who see it begin to mock him, saying 'This man began to build and was not able to finish'?" Luke 14:28-30*

This verse explains the importance of having a budget and planning. To know in advance your expenses so that you can properly prepare and save. Those without a budget tend to spend sporadically and frivolously, and therefore will not be a good money manager.

As we look further into money managers, Luke 16 illustrates another parable of Jesus. This one being about an unscrupulous money manager. There are several lessons in this passage. It reads,

> *Now He was also saying to the disciples, "There was a rich man who had a manager, and this manager was reported to him as squandering his possessions. And he called him and said to him, 'What is this I hear about you? Give an accounting of your management, for you can no longer be manager.'*

This manager was not incompetent, he was crooked. He was entrusted with the wealth of the rich man but had ulterior motives.

> *The manager said to himself, 'What shall I do, since my master is taking the management away from me? I am not strong enough to dig; I am ashamed to beg. I know what I shall do, so that when I am removed from the management*

people will welcome me into their homes.

Even after being caught and confronted, he didn't care about his boss. He immediately switched gears into survival mode. Apparently, he wasn't the outdoor/blue collar type, and his lifestyle must've been so that he had too much pride to beg on the street.

And he summoned each one of his master's debtors, and he began saying to the first, 'How much do you owe my master?' And he said, 'A hundred measures of oil.' And he said to him, 'Take your bill, and sit down quickly and write fifty.' Then he said to another, 'And how much do you owe?' And he said, 'A hundred measures of wheat.' He said to him, 'Take your bill, and write eighty.' And his master praised the unrighteous manager because he had acted shrewdly; for the sons of this age are more shrewd in relation to their own kind than the sons of light. And I say to you, make friends for yourselves by means of the wealth of unrighteousness, so that when it fails, they will receive you into the eternal dwellings.

What he did was not moral or ethical. He was still cheating his boss and looking out for his own interest by discounting the debtors to get in their good graces. However, his master praised his shrewdness. The lesson in this tells us people in the world can be shrewder than believers. They are savvy with their investments and how they manage money. This manager was cunning when it came to self-preservation.

With his back against a wall, the money manager found a way to use his resources. Christians should also use God's resources wisely. When we do, we are able to benefit the kingdom.

"He who is faithful in a very little thing is faithful also in much; and he who is unrighteous in a very little thing is

unrighteous also in much. Therefore, if you have not been faithful in the use of unrighteous wealth, who will entrust the true riches to you? And if you have not been faithful in the use of that which is another's, who will give you that which is your own?

Real estate, businesses, or the stock market. How are you investing your money?

What savvy plans do you have with the money God entrusts with you that will ultimately benefit the kingdom and bring Him glory?

Most people spend more time planning their next vacation than they do their financial future!

How much thought have you put into your monthly budget, your annual budget? Your retirement? Your estate?

The Righteous Rich:

Wealth is not proof of righteousness. Amos would describe there being two classes, a "righteous poor" and a "wicked rich." However, if we look at the old testament, there is a positive connection between the "righteous" and the "rich." Abraham, Isaac, Jacob, Joseph, David, Solomon, Job, etc. all had means and lived in abundance. Although one doesn't necessary imply the other, we can see how God used these men to bless others. Riches from God were never meant to stop with one person, but to pass through us.

Abraham is not only known as the Father of Faith, but he is the first person in the bible connecting God's blessing with righteousness and riches.

Now Abram was very rich in livestock, in silver and in gold.
Genesis 13:2.

Not only was Abram blessed but it was expected of him to be a blessing to others by spreading the wealth.

Now the Lord said to Abram, "Go forth from your country, and from your relatives and from your father's house, to the land which I will show you; and I will make you a great nation, and I will bless you, and make your name great; and so you shall be a blessing; and I will bless those who bless you, and the one who curses you I will curse, and in you all the families of the earth will be blessed."

If there are no righteous men with riches, how does God circulate money where it needs to be?

God wants righteous men in positions of authority. Men who can be trusted with his assets, but also have the know-how. Money has always been a bi product of the blessing. Money by itself is neutral and can be used for good or bad, but when we talk about being on assignment for the Kingdom of God, you can expect the resources to follow God's will.

Key Takeaways:

1. We will never be the owner of God's possessions, but He allows us to manage, protect and expand his assets.

2. Money management has spiritual significance. The power and

meaning we give to our money reflect how we manage our lives.

3. Wealth is not built over night but over time.
We can learn a lot from an ant.

4. We're all given time, talents or treasures to work
with, and God expects a return on His investment.
Each will be given according to our ability.

5. With God's wisdom, Joseph was able to implement
a strategy for Egypt to survive through a famine.
He understood how to manage assets.

6. Saving and investing is not only recommended, but
expected, and if done correct there should be enough
to pass along to your children's children.

7. To manage money you need a blueprint,
or a budget to operate from.

8. A Christian should be as savvy as the unbeliever. Be creative
and ask God for innovative ways to earn and invest money.

9. Wealth is not proof of righteousness, but there is an interesting
connection between prominent characters in the old testament
who were considered righteous and who also happened to be rich.

C. HONORING GOD
WITH OUR MONEY

9. THE HEART OF GIVING

In everything I showed you that by working hard in this manner you must help the weak and remember the words of the Lord Jesus, that He Himself said, 'It is more blessed to give than to receive. Acts 20:35

Hopefully, we've established a core foundation of God being the Source of all riches, wealth, and prosperity. The earth is His and the fullness thereof (Psalm 24:1). We will never own it, but we are allowed to manage it. He gives us the power to get wealth (Deuteronomy 8:18).

Most Christians don't have a problem understanding the concept that God is the Creator, and the Source of all things. We as believers often ask for God's wisdom and guidance when it comes to attaining wealth, but more than likely we have not relinquished our control over money matters. The root of the issue is trust.

Do we truly believe that God has provided for us, and will continue to do so?

Making a purchase is as much an emotional transaction as it is for goods and services. We are attached to what we put our money toward. We love the things so much that we aspire to acquire more and more of it. We work hard at our jobs to be compensated with pay that purchases the luxury items that our flesh desires. We feel justified in our spending. We say, why not? I'm the one who worked hard for it.

In this area, the most devoted Christian has a conflict of interest. We allow God's reign in every area except the wallet. We want to make our own spending decisions because we feel that we've labored and toiled for it.

The more we understand the freedom in allowing God to assist with our executive spending decisions, the more we can see the fullness of what a relationship with God will do. Those who have money in abundance and give, likely give according to their surplus or confidence in their ability to produce more money. Most give based on their excess, but God looks at who gives out of their whole.

Are you aware that the Kingdom of God has its own economy? How does it differ from the earthly economy?

What is economics?

Economics is the branch of knowledge concerned with the production, consumption, exchange of goods and services and transfer of wealth. The condition of a region or group regarding material prosperity. In the Bible, we're told to seek first the Kingdom.

According to this, the Christian definition would likely say: Economics is the branch of knowledge concerned with the production, consumption, exchange of goods and services and transfer of wealth "as a steward under the authority of the Holy Spirit."

The Kingdom's economy does not make sense to our earthly economy. In the Kingdom economy, we are told: *It is better to give than receive (Acts 20:35). Your possessions are not your own (Acts 4:32). Don't lay-up treasures on earth but in heaven (Matthew 6:19-20).*

In this section, we will discuss honoring God with our money. The heart of giving is not automatic and must be learned by most.

Some may say that children are naturally inclined to act selfishly. As we understand the emotional attachment to our purchases, we tend to ignore God's instructions on giving. As we learn the Word of God and begin to take steps of faith toward giving, we allow God 100% access into our world, and we have an unhindered, unlimited experience with God that we may never have otherwise.

Lesson of the Widow's Mite

> *And He sat down opposite the treasury, and began observing how the people were putting money into the treasury; and many rich people were putting in large sums. A poor widow came and put in two small copper coins, which amount to a cent. Calling His disciples to Him, He said to them, "Truly I say to you, this poor widow put in more than all the contributors to the treasury; for they all put in out of their surplus, but she, out of her poverty, put in all she owned, all she had to live on." Mark 12:41-44*

In God's eyes this poor widow gave more than all the others put together. The two small coins had no real earthly value, it was by far the least given compared to everyone else. However, her giving was measured by her heart. She was likely not even noticed by others, but Jesus noticed her. The wealthy gave out of their surplus (after all the bills and discretionary spending), but she gave out of her poverty.

Have you ever given your very last because you felt that's what God wanted? What was the result?

> *You will be enriched in every way so that you can be generous on every occasion, and through us your generosity will result in thanksgiving to God. 2 Corinthians 9:11*

Here Paul is basically saying God can and will multiply your giving. God is looking for distribution centers who are willing to be used as a conduit to spread financial blessings. Enriched in every way is an example of a double-sided blessing, that not only results in praise by the receiver, but allows the giver to feel enriched.

> *But who am I, and who are my people, that we should be able to give as generously as this? Everything comes from you, and we have given you only what comes from your hand. 1 Chronicles 29:14*

When we give to God, we are simply giving back a portion of what He has first given us. David recognizes the source of it all.

Imagine being an ambassador who moves to another country as a representative of our kingdom. All expenses, including travel, housing, food, and even entertainment, are paid by the kingdom we represent. Although the ambassador doesn't own any of the property and can't claim any of the assets, we are allowed full access. We're also given authority to make executive decisions on behalf of our kingdom.

A Christian, on earth, is simply an ambassador. We have been given the authority by God to represent the kingdom. We are entrusted by God to make executive decisions on behalf of the kingdom. In this position, we're able to benefit from the livelihood our kingdom provides. Our house, car, gas, food, and entertainment are all provided. We realize we will never be the owner, but we are content in knowing our needs are taken care of.

> Now the man had relations with his wife Eve, and she conceived and gave birth to Cain, and she said, "I have gotten a man-child with the help of the Lord." Again, she gave birth to his brother Abel. And Abel was a keeper of flocks, but Cain was a tiller of the ground. So, it came about in the course of time that Cain brought an offering to the Lord of the fruit of the ground. Abel, on his part also brought of the firstlings of his flock and of their fat portions. And the Lord had regard for Abel and for his offering; but for Cain and for his offering He had no regard. So, Cain became very angry and his countenance fell. Then the Lord said to Cain, "Why are you angry? And why has your countenance fallen? If you do well, will not your countenance be lifted up? And if you do not do well, sin is crouching at the door; and its desire is for you, but you must master it." Cain told Abel his brother. And it came about when they were in the field, that Cain rose up against Abel his brother and killed him. Genesis 4:1-8

The first account of giving in the Bible comes from Cain and Abel. Abel brought the fat portions of the firstborn of his flock. He gave his first and the best of what he had. God looked with favor on Abel and his offering.

What is the difference between the heart of Cain and Abel in regard to their giving?

God evaluates the motives of each person's giving. The Bible doesn't say why God had no regard for Cain's offering. It may have been his motive or attitude.

What can we learn from Cain? What can we learn from Abel?

Abel gave his first and his best. In Proverbs, it says

> *Honor the Lord from your wealth and from the first of all your produce, so your barns will be filled with plenty and your vats will overflow with new wine. Proverbs 3:9-10*

Why does Solomon say this? What is significant about the first of all our produce?

Why do we give in the first place if God is the Provider and He will give us something in return?

This is the heart of God displaying the joy of giving. He is a natural giver. There is joy in Him giving and I believe He wants us to share in this joy of giving with Him.

> *A man may give freely, and still his wealth will be increased; and another may keep back more than is right, but only comes to be in need. Proverbs 11:24-25*

Even if you restrict your giving, you will still be in need.

> *And if I give all my possessions to feed the poor, and if I surrender my body to be burned, but do not have love, it profits me nothing. 1 Corinthians 13:3*

This deals with the intentions of the heart and the motives behind giving. If we are giving because it's good publicity or we want to show off, then the true joy of giving is short-lived.

> *For where your treasure is, there your heart will be also.*
> *Matthew 6:21*

Why are you giving?

What are the motives behind your giving?

Do you give to receive or to be seen?

Do you give out of your surplus, or do you give out of your whole?

Do you give when you know God is trying to stretch your faith?

How much control do you allow God in the area of finances?

The Bible is neither for or against money, but what's more important is our heart condition and stewardship. God's perspective on prosperity differs from today's culture. True riches are based on a spiritual value system. Those without lots of money are challenged with being envious of those with much more money. Those who have more money are challenged with being arrogant. There may be a person who likes to give, but they gain money dishonestly. One may be an honest worker, but in serious debt. The other may be completely debt free but isn't a giver. We must all rely on God to have the heart of a good steward.

What does the Bible say about tithing (one tenth)?

Regardless of denomination or time in the faith, even most seasoned believers disagree on the topic of tithing.

Is tithing still required?

Must we really give 10% of our income?

What counts as income?

Do we give from our net or gross?

Tithing was a part of the Mosaic covenant. The New Testament states we are no longer under the Mosaic covenant. *(Galatians 3:15-25, Romans 7:7-25, Hebrews 9-10)*

The first mention of tithe in *Genesis 14* says:

> *He blessed him and said, blessed be Abram of God Most High, possessor of heaven and earth; And blessed be God Most High, who has delivered your enemies into your hand." He gave him a tenth of all. Genesis 14:19-20.*

God told Abram through Melchizedek that there is no king on earth more powerful than him. After the blessing, Abram gave a tenth of his spoils to Melchizedek. Please note, he did not give to get something in return. He gave in response to all God had done.

Second mention of tithe came in *Genesis 28.*

> *Then Jacob took an oath, and said, If God will be with me, and keep me safe on my journey, and give me food and clothing to put on, so that I come again to my father's house in peace, then I will take the Lord to be my God, and this stone which I have put up for a pillar will be God's house:*

and of all you give me, I will give a tenth part to you. Genesis 28:20-22

Abram gave to Melchizedek, and Jacob gave to God, but those were one-time, temporary events. There's no indication that their tithing was done regularly, nor is there a universal command given to believers to tithe from the passages.

After the first two examples, the tithe was later made official under the Law that God gave to all of Israel through Moses *(Leviticus 27:30-33, Numbers 18:20-32, Deuteronomy 14:22-29, Deuteronomy 26:12-15).*

The tithe was used to support the Levitical priesthood and the temple/tabernacle. The Levites, unlike the other eleven tribes of Israel did not receive an allocated portion of the land of Canaan for their possession.

> *In addition, he gave orders to the people of Jerusalem to give to the priests and Levites that part which was theirs by right, so that they might be strong in keeping the law of the Lord. And when the order was made public, straight away the children of Israel gave, in great amounts, the first-fruits of their grain and wine and oil and honey, and of the produce of their fields; and they took in a tenth part of everything, a great store. 2 Chronicles 31:4-5*

In my opinion, as God was recognized as being the ultimate source of the wealth that was received, a portion was given back to God (through his appointed ministers), one-tenth in thanksgiving to Him.

In fact, God commanded the Israelites to tithe. By giving back a portion of what God had provided, they recognized his sovereignty while demonstrating faith in God to continue to be their source. By doing this, the Israelites came under the covenant.

> *Will a man keep back from God what is right? But you have kept back what is mine. But you say, what have we kept back from you? Tenths and offerings. You are cursed with a curse; for you have kept back from me what is mine, even all this nation. Let your tenths come into the store-house so that there may be food in my house, and put me to the test by doing so, says the Lord of armies, and see if I do not make the windows of heaven open and send down such a blessing on you that there is no room for it. And on your account, I will keep back the locusts from wasting the fruits of your land; and the fruit of your vine will not be dropped on the field before its time, says the Lord of armies and you will be named happy by all nations: for you will be a land of delight, says the Lord of armies. Malachi 3:8-12*

Today, by order of Melchizedek, Jesus is our Great King and High Priest, (Hebrews 5:5), and there are no longer any tabernacles or temples.

Do you know what replaced the temple?

The temple that was designed by David and built by Solomon was only a representation, but since Jesus, that temple now resides in us.

> *Or do you not know that your body is a temple of the Holy Spirit who is in you, whom you have from God, and that you are not your own? For you have been bought with a*

price: therefore, glorify God in your body. (1 Corinthians 6:19-20)

I would say that tithing is no longer required as it was according to the Mosaic covenant. HOWEVER, as we continue this study, we'll learn that the new testament focuses on sacrificial and generous giving. This removes the simple cookie cutter measurement of giving, and replaces it with a pure heart of giving, which we're told will increase our joy. The one-time God says "test me" in the Bible is related to our giving. God clearly wants us to be givers!

2 Corinthians 9:7 (NIV) says,

> *"Each of you should give what you have decided in your heart to give, not reluctantly or under compulsion, for God loves a cheerful giver."*

There is much that we can learn about giving. Most of Jesus' parables related to money are based on giving.

Other scriptures in the Old Testament regarding the tithe are:

Deuteronomy 14:28-29, Nehemiah 10:35-37, Amos 4:4-5, Deuteronomy 12:5-6, and *Leviticus 27:30-34.*

Keep in mind that tithing is still practiced in today's church. The Old Testament scriptures of tithing (10%) have created a base line for today's giving to the church. The donations received are meant to support its ministers, as well as the poor, widows, and orphans.

I encourage us not to be so technical about "giving of our money" that we overlook the purpose and the heart condition of giving. Jesus says to the scribes and Pharisees in Matthew 23:23, who were extremely legalistic in the smallest details of the law, that they were overlooking the bigger picture and more important matters of the law such as justice, mercy and faithfulness.

What are offerings?

An offering is in addition to the tithe. It comes from what's left over after you've taken care of your obligations (bills, etc.).

Do I give from my net or gross?

Remember, we should be giving because we want to and not because we have to. The heart of giving is much more important than us legalizing this action. Giving from your gross is technically the first fruit because it is giving to God even before Uncle Sam takes his portion.

> Honor the Lord with your wealth, with the first fruits of all your crops. Proverbs 3:9

What does your heart say to do?

Should I tithe while in debt?

As we've learned, God doesn't want us to owe anyone (but to love them), because it limits our resources to do His will (we are slaves to our lenders). However, by giving to God, we are recognizing His majesty and sovereignty, as well as His ability to provide for all of our needs. If we understand the balance of God as the provider, while being serious about debt cancellation, I believe God will give us direction on how to balance them both until we are free and clear.

I'd say that God would not want us to stop giving, even in debt. What is probably more important to look at is the frivolous spending that we can be guilty of. To neglect God and turn around and spend frivolously is not being a good steward.

As we continue to look at the New Testament, we can approach our understanding of giving as a heart condition. In Matthew, it reads:

> Give, and it will be given to you. They will pour into your lap a good measure—pressed down, shaken together, and running over. For by your standard of measure it will be measured to you in return." Luke 6:38

If our heart is right, our giving has no choice but to come back in abundance. This is the law of sowing in effect.

> Give to him who asks you, and from him who wants to borrow from you do not turn away. Matthew 5:42

God wants us to be lenders and not borrowers. We have also been charged to love our neighbors as ourselves.

This does not mean be foolish and give from what we cannot afford. Christian giving should have the heart to be done without the expectation of return (unless it's an agreement). Either way, I'd be mindful of sowing into bad soil. Deep down I believe we already know when these situations arise.

> But love your enemies, do good, and lend, hoping for nothing in return; and your reward will be great, and you will be sons of the Most-High. Luke 6:35

Each of you should give what you have decided in your heart to give, not reluctantly or under compulsion, for God loves a cheerful giver. 2 Corinthians 9:7

This is the heart of giving. You should not be in the middle of service having a mental tug of war. Honestly, giving more takes more faith, but we should look at whom we are giving and allow that to settle in our hearts the amount of the gift.

So, when you give to the needy, do not announce it with trumpets, as the hypocrites do in the synagogues and on the streets, to be honored by others. Truly I tell you, they have received their reward in full. Matthew 6:2

We ruin the gift when we broadcast it for publicity. There is a personal joy in giving. Let that be enough. At the end of the day, God is the source of it. What can we really take credit for?

This is not why we give, but it should definitely be reassuring. There are so many other examples of giving -that's not about money, but is still from the heart:

A generous person will prosper; whoever refreshes others will be refreshed. Proverbs 11:25

1. Ruth devotes her life to Naomi *(Ruth 1)*
2. Joseph of Arimathea gives Jesus his tomb, an expensive and irreplaceable gift *(Matthew 27:57-60)*
3. Jesus washes his disciples' feet *(John 13:1-17)*
4. God sent his Son to die for our sins *(John 3:16)*

◆ ◆ ◆

Key Takeaways:

1. It's much better to give than to receive.

2. The economics of the Kingdom of God is much different than the economics of this world. What God requires does not make sense to the non-believer.

3. Giving from the heart is valued much more than the size of the gift. A poor person giving from their whole supersedes a rich person giving from their surplus.

4. Tithing was a part of the Mosaic covenant, which we are not technically under today. However, some churches use Old Testament law as a baseline to give toward the church ministry as well as the poor, widows and orphans.

5. Not tithing should not be a license to not give at all. It's ultimately a heart condition. Don't give out of what's left, but first give from the heart, God's will to be done.

6. Don't be so legalistic about one aspect of the law, tithing, that you forget todays commandment of loving the Lord God with all your heart (which includes your finances) and loving your neighbor as yourself. This should allow us the freedom to give.

10. GREAT GENEROSITY

I n 2 Corinthians 8 Paul is writing from Macedonia to the Corinthians in hopes of encouraging the church to not only give freely but to unite and solve their problems.

Now, brethren, we wish to make known to you the grace of God which has been given in the churches of Macedonia, 2 that in a great ordeal of affliction their abundance of joy and their deep poverty overflowed in the wealth of their liberality. 3 For I testify that according to their ability, and beyond their ability, they gave of their own accord, 4 begging us with much urging for the favor of participation in the support of the saints, 5 and this, not as we had expected, but they first gave themselves to the Lord and to us by the will of God. 6 So we urged Titus that as he had previously made a beginning, so he would also complete in you this gracious work as well.

The Macedonian churches (in Phillipi, Thessalonica, and Barea) were poor people. They had given even more than Paul expected because they wanted to help. At the heart of giving, the amount is not the focus. What they gave was sacrificial. They did not give grudgingly or out of necessity. It was simply the good and right thing to do.

How does our giving compare to the Macedonians?

7 But just as you abound in everything, in faith and utterance and knowledge and in all earnestness and in the love we inspired in you, see that you abound in this gracious work also. 8 I am not speaking this as a command, but as proving through the earnestness of others the sincerity of your love also.

Again, we should never feel coerced, brow-beaten or given a guilt-trip to give. Nor should we use money as some sort of bribe or tip jar for Jesus in expectation of a large blessing. This is not Las Vegas or the stock market. Giving in this capacity will only disappoint and frustrate you.

Do nothing from selfishness or empty conceit, but with humility of mind regard one another as more important than yourselves. Philippians 2:3

What Paul expressed to the Corinthians was not a command, but a challenge to prove their love was sincere. The Corinthian believers had excelled in faith, good preaching (speech), much knowledge and sincere and intense conviction, as well as love. Paul wanted them to also be front-runners in giving.

9 For you know the grace of our Lord Jesus Christ, that though He was rich, yet for your sake He became poor, so that you through His poverty might become rich.

We should be motivated by (internal) love not by (external) pressure. Jesus sacrificed his heavenly glory and rights of His position to become "nothing," while taking the very nature of a servant, in the likeness of humanity.

Philippians 2:7, so that we may become rich, by and through him to receive salvation and everlasting life with God.

10 I give my opinion in this matter, for this is to your advantage, who were the first to begin a year ago not only to do this, but also to desire to do it. 11 But now finish doing it also, so that just as there was the readiness to desire it, so there may be also the completion of it by your ability.

Paul is asking them to fulfill a promise they made a year ago, which was to collect money for the churches in Jerusalem (apparently, they already had money). By doing so it would only benefit them in the future.

12 For if the readiness is present, it is acceptable according to what a person has, not according to what he does not have. 13 For this is not for the ease of others and for your affliction, but by way of equality— 14 at this present time your abundance being a supply for their need, so that their abundance also may become a supply for your need, that there may be equality; 15 as it is written, "He who gathered much did not have too much, and he who gathered little had no lack."

We should be praying about what we decide to give. When we make promises of financial support, we should follow through on those promises, using God as the filter by which we give.

God was able to provide manna for the Israelites in the wilderness. Today, He uses people to help other people. By our giving, God is able to reach others in this earthly realm to cover certain earthly needs.

We should also be giving from the heart, and not out of our excess or surplus. At the same time, you cannot give something you don't have. Although it sounds good, this is the same thought process that gets us tangled up in debt. Our desires overrule our wisdom and we buy things (with credit cards) that we cannot afford or do not have the money to pay for today.

16 But thanks be to God who puts the same earnestness on your behalf in the heart of Titus. 17 For he not only accepted our appeal, but being himself very earnest, he has gone to you of his own accord. 18 We have sent along with him the brother whose fame in the things of the gospel has spread through all the churches; 19 and not only this, but he has also been appointed by the churches to travel with us in this gracious work, which is being administered by us for the glory of the Lord Himself, and to show our readiness, 20 taking precaution so that no one will discredit us in our administration of this generous gift; 21 for we have regard for what is honorable, not only in the sight of the Lord, but also in the sight of men. 22 We have sent with them our brother, whom we have often tested and found diligent in many things, but now even more diligent because of his great confidence in you. 23 As for Titus, he is my partner and fellow worker among you; as for our brethren, they are messengers of the churches, a glory to Christ. 24 Therefore openly before the churches, show them the proof of your love and of our reason for boasting about you.

Financial matters should be handled above reproach. This section of scripture talks about the integrity of those assigned for this task of collecting such a large amount of money to be distributed in Jerusalem. They wanted to be clear and transparent in their actions, removing all suspicion. It is important for the church to know that those handling the money of the church will not misuse it.

In conclusion, we should be mindful of God and the kingdom's economics. It is a system to support the church and ministry of Christ, as the church is in position to support those in need.

> *Be devoted to one another in brotherly love; give preference to one another in honor. Romans 12:10*

Key Takeaways:

1. Our willingness to give cheerfully is more important than the amount we give.

2. As believers, we should follow through on our promises of financial commitment.

3. We should give as much as we are able.

4. In the Kingdom's economy, if you give to support another in need, others will give to support you in your need.

5. We should give with Christ in mind, as a response to all He has done.

6. Giving to receive, as if you are placing a wager or playing the stock market is the wrong motive and usually results in disappointment and frustration.

7. Sacrificial giving must also be responsibly handled. We shouldn't give so much that we neglect our homes and dependents.

8. Financial matters should be handled above reproach. Those in the church responsible for handling the finances should be transparent, operate in integrity, and do so with extreme care.

11. THE INDESCRIBABLE GIFT

In 2 Corinthians 9, it reads:

For it is superfluous for me to write to you about this ministry to the saints; 2 for I know your readiness, of which I boast about you to the Macedonians, namely, that Achaia has been prepared since last year, and your zeal has stirred up most of them. 3 But I have sent the brethren, in order that our boasting about you may not be made empty in this case, so that, as I was saying, you may be prepared; 4 otherwise if any Macedonians come with me and find you unprepared, we—not to speak of you—will be put to shame by this confidence. 5 So I thought it necessary to urge the brethren that they would go on ahead to you and arrange beforehand your previously promised bountiful gift, so that the same would be ready as a bountiful gift and not affected by covetousness.

Paul reminded the church of their commitment to bless the churches in Jerusalem with a financial gift. He sent men ahead to make sure the gift was prepared and not seem like a last-minute, on-the-spot, pressure tactic to give.

> 6 Now this I say, he who sows sparingly will also reap sparingly, and he who sows bountifully will also reap bountifully. 7 Each one must do just as he has purposed in his heart, not grudgingly or under compulsion, for God loves a cheerful giver. 8 And God is able to make all grace abound to you, so that always having all sufficiency in everything, you may have an abundance for every good deed;

We should be prayerful about our gifts before we write the check or walk in the church. It should be something a husband and wife discuss and settle so that both are on one accord. By the time you get to the actual act of giving, you can rejoice and feel good about your participation in this form of worship to God.
Its natural to feel if we give generously that we won't have enough to meet our needs. This verse explains Kingdom economics in that God is able to meet all of our needs because He is the source. He is also on our side, and who we're giving to. With this in mind, we should realize that what we give will be mirrored or measured back to us.

Remember that giving is a heart condition. Be prayerful and don't let the external noise distract you. If you keep your giving sacred between you and God, with the right heart to give, you will never be in lack. In fact, the trust you exhibit will always be reciprocated, with more. You cannot beat God's giving, no matter how hard you try!

The amount of the gift is not as important as the heart behind the gift. According to this, we are blessed in proportion.

9 as it is written, "He scattered abroad, he gave to the poor, His righteousness endures forever." 10 Now He who supplies seed to the sower and bread for food will supply and multiply your seed for sowing and increase the harvest of your righteousness; 11 you will be enriched in everything for all liberality, which through us is producing thanksgiving to God.

God gives us the resources to invest and reap returns, which we ultimately offer back to Him through our giving. It's a cycle, and a flow. This illustration gives us encouragement to stay within the flow of money by not allowing it to cause a log jam by hoarding or fear of lack, but of freely giving and being generous.

If there is a flow to money, how do we interrupt that flow?

What actions cause us to get out of the cycle of money?

Giving does so much more for the giver than the receiver. This is just one clear example of how you can never out-give God. The laws of sowing and reaping will always overwhelm you. And yes, this is a law!

12 For the ministry of this service is not only fully supplying the needs of the saints, but is also overflowing through many thanksgivings to God. 13 Because of the proof given by this ministry, they will glorify God for your obedience to your confession of the gospel of Christ and for the liberality of your contribution to them and to all, 14 while they also, by prayer on your behalf, yearn for you because of the surpassing grace of God in you. 15 Thanks be to God for His indescribable gift!

The ministry is proof of God's goodness. As a result of this goodness, those in receipt of the gift will be thankful and glorify God for His generosity. In your giving to others, have you witnessed how God gets the glory? There are also spiritual rewards for our generosity, which we will discuss in the next section.

Key Takeaways:

1. Prepare your gift. Pray with your spouse and settle it before you write the check or walk into the church. By settling the amount ahead of time, you can enter into worship instead of dealing with pressure or compulsion.

2. Your giving is always reciprocated. You can never out-give to God and not reap a harvest in return.

3. Stay within the flow of money. God creates the seed for us to invest and reap a harvest. As we give back in honor to Him, he continues to reproduce, recycle and replenish the seed, so we can receive and give more. This is Kingdom economics.

4. The ministry is proof of God's goodness, and because of our giving, the recipients are thankful and glorify the Lord. In addition, as givers, there is an eternal return on our giving that we will one day realize.

12. STORING UP YOUR TREASURE

"Do not lay up for yourselves treasures on earth, where moth and rust destroy and where thieves break in and steal, but lay up for yourselves treasures in heaven, where neither moth nor rust destroys and where thieves do not break in and steal. For where your treasure is, there your heart will be also." Matthew 6:20

I saw a post on Facebook about a forty-year-old fashion blogger, diagnosed with stage four cancer. Since chemo and radiation were not working the way she had hoped, she discontinued the treatments so she could "enjoy the rest of her time with friends and family and be as pain-free as possible."

To her half-a-million followers on IG she said this:
"I have a brand-new car parked outside that can't do anything for me, I have all kinds of designer-clothes, shoes and bags that can't do anything for me, I have money in my account that can't do anything for me, I have a big well-furnished house that can't do anything for me.

Look, I'm lying here in a twin size hospital bed; I can take a plane any day of the week if I like, but that can't do anything for me. So, do not let anyone make u feel bad for the things you don't have - but the things u have, be happy with those; if you have a roof over your head who cares what kind of furniture is in it... the most important thing in life is LOVE"

"I'm not sure of this fashion bloggers belief in God, Jesus or Heaven, but regardless of her religious convictions, the reality of death caused her to reflect on the things that matter the most. If you knew the time/day that you were going to expire, what would you want to have accomplished?"

As we think about our transition, money seems to become less and less significant. We spend our days chasing dollar signs and acquiring wealth, but is it all in vain?

As it relates to money, I've never seen a suitcase at a funeral, nor have I ever seen a U-Haul truck follow a hearse to a cemetery, because we all know that you can't bring anything with you on your trip to the afterlife.

What does it profit a man to gain the world and lose his soul? If we're cognizant of this, wisdom should tell us that we need to make preparations for eternity. As we've read in *James 4*,

> *"...you do not know what tomorrow will bring. What is your life? For you are a mist that appears for a little time and then vanishes."*

Tomorrow is not promised to anyone! In fact, as soon as we are born our timeline on earth has already begun the countdown.

In *John 14:3* Jesus talks of a place,

"My Father's house has many rooms; if that were not so, would I have told you that I am going there to prepare a place for you? 3 And if I go and prepare a place for you, I will come back and take you to be with me that you also may be where I am.

Earthly wealth can be misleading. The Israelites show us how attaining worldly wealth can cloud our judgement and compromise our relationship with God.

For when I bring them into the land flowing with milk and honey, which I swore to their fathers, and they have eaten and are satisfied and become prosperous, then they will turn to other gods and serve them, and spurn Me and break My covenant. Deuteronomy 31:20

We cannot afford to live in the here and now and ignore what is to come. Life on earth as we know it is but a blink.

Is God your personal genie? Are you only worried about receiving the next wish? Thinking of God in this manner is dangerously deceiving.

How often do you think about your heavenly future?

We carefully plan our education, we prepare for the arrival of our children, we prepare for retirement, and even prepare for a weekend vacation, but how do we prepare for Heaven?

Besides receiving salvation, what have you done to prepare for eternity?

Jesus says store up our treasures in heaven. Matthew 6:20.

He then says our treasures in heaven are directly linked to our hearts. For where your treasures are, your heart will be also. Matthew 6:21.

The Bible mentions rewards in heaven for the believer who serves faithfully.

Whoever welcomes a prophet as a prophet will receive a prophet's reward, and whoever welcomes a righteous person as a righteous person will receive a righteous person's reward and if anyone gives even a cup of cold water to one of these little ones who is my disciple, truly I tell you, that person will certainly not lose their reward. Matthew 10:41-42

Jesus even talks about returning with rewards in *Revelations 22:12,*

"Behold, I am coming soon, bringing my recompense with me to repay each one for what he has done."

There are five crowns mentioned in the scripture that we can also potentially receive:

The Crown of Life *(Revelations 2:10)* This crown is for all believers, but is especially dear to those who endure sufferings, who bravely confront persecution for Jesus, even to the point of death

The Imperishable Crown *(1 Corinthians 9:24-25)* that wreath of leaves that was soon to turn brittle and fall apart. But not so the heavenly crown; faithful endurance wins a heavenly reward which is incorruptible

The Crown of Righteousness *(2 Timothy 4:8)* We inherit this crown through the righteousness of Christ which is what gives us a right to it

The Crown of Glory *(1 Peter 5:4)* crown will be awarded to all those who long for or love His appearing.

The Crown of Rejoicing *(1 Thessalonians 2:19)* our reward where "God will wipe away every tear . . . there shall be no more death, nor sorrow, nor crying.

God wants us to prosper on earth, but not at the expense of our souls and eternity. Money may buy many things, but it's useless in Heaven. We must stay in remembrance of "who we are, whose we are, where we are from," and "what we represent." Our purpose here on earth cannot and should not be defined by our bank accounts.

> *But you, be sober in all things, endure hardship, do the work of an evangelist, fulfill your ministry. For I am already being poured out like a drink offering, and the time of my departure is at hand. I have fought the good fight, I have finished the race, I have kept the faith. From now on the crown of righteousness is laid up for me, which the Lord, the righteous judge, will award to me on that day—and not only to me, but to all who crave His appearing. 2 Timothy 4:5-8*

Is it possible to live a full life and never receive the promises of God?

> *All these died in faith, without receiving the promises,*

but having seen them and having welcomed them from a distance, and having confessed that they were strangers and exiles on the earth. Hebrews 11:13

Although they could've given up, they finished their course, because they knew what was to come. There is a saying, Y.O.L.O. (you only live once). That is far from the truth, but the reality is some would rather trade-in the unseen future (heaven) to live their dream now, temporarily (on earth). Would that be worth it for you?

Do you seek the approval of man? If so, your reward will be here and now. Do you use your gifts and talents for the kingdom, or for your own personal gain and desires? If so, your reward will be here and now. Have you short-changed your future inheritance for a few crumbs today?

> *"The man who plants and the man who waters have one purpose, and each will be rewarded according to his own labor" 1 Corinthians 3:8*

Are you invested in the kingdom's economy? Are you involved in the ministry of winning souls for Christ? Or is it all about you and yours, and no more?

If God blessed you with millions of dollars, then one day told you to give it all away, would you do it?

How secure is your relationship with Christ to drop all you have and follow Him on the drop of a dime?

> *And as he was setting out on his journey, a man ran up and knelt before him and asked him, "Good Teacher, what must I do to inherit eternal life?" And Jesus said to him, "*

Why do you call me good? No one is good except God alone. You know the commandments: 'Do not murder, do not commit adultery, do not steal, do not bear false witness, do not defraud, honor your father and mother.'" And he said to him, "Teacher, all these I have kept from my youth." And Jesus, looking at him, loved him, and said to him, "You lack one thing: go, sell all that you have and give to the poor, and you will have treasure in heaven; and come, follow me." Disheartened by the saying, he went away sorrowful, for he had great possessions. And Jesus looked around and said to his disciples, "How difficult it will be for those who have wealth to enter the kingdom of God!" And the disciples were amazed at his words. But Jesus said to them again, "Children, how difficult it is to enter the kingdom of God! It is easier for a camel to go through the eye of a needle than for a rich person to enter the kingdom of God." And they were exceedingly astonished, and said to him, "Then who can be saved?" Jesus looked at them and said, "With man it is impossible, but not with God. For all things are possible with God." Peter began to say to him, "See, we have left everything and followed you." Jesus said, "Truly, I say to you, there is no one who has left house or brothers or sisters or mother or father or children or lands, for my sake and for the gospel, who will not receive a hundredfold now in this time, houses and brothers and sisters and mothers and children and lands, with persecutions, and in the age to come eternal life. But many who are first will be last, and the last first." Mark 10:17-31

This rich young ruler wanted to know how to enter heaven, as well as gain inheritance rewards. He was wise in knowing that there was a bigger picture, but not wise enough to see the opportunity Jesus presented him with.

The disciples forfeited prominent careers to follow Jesus. I'm not sure if they knew how extraordinary their decision was at that time, but their lives would never be the same. Although they endured trials on earth and suffered horrible deaths for the Gospel, their inheritance far exceeded their sacrifice.

What are you willing to sacrifice for the Gospel?

Knowing now what the disciples didn't know when they accepted their calling, how can you take advantage of their experiences to benefit your future?

This rich young ruler was naïve to think he kept all of God's commands.

Is it possible to be so caught in religious routine that we overlook what's truly important to God?

Pride so easily befalls us that before we even realize it, we are outside of God's will. Daily we must humble ourselves and seek God's face. The last thing we want to be is lukewarm, or salt that loses its saltiness. If we can't be used by God, then we are useless.

The goal of a Christian is to hear six words: "Well done, my good and faithful servant."

Have you ever asked God how you can achieve this goal?

Selfish desires of the flesh seek earthly rewards, but the spirit seeks eternal rewards. Jesus gives an illustration of how this can be accomplished.

> *Then the King will say to those on His right, 'Come, you who are blessed of My Father, inherit the kingdom prepared for you from the foundation of the world. For I was hun-*

gry, and you gave Me something to eat; I was thirsty, and you gave Me something to drink; I was a stranger, and you invited Me in; naked, and you clothed Me; I was sick, and you visited Me; I was in prison, and you came to Me.' Then the righteous will answer Him, 'Lord, when did we see You hungry, and feed You, or thirsty, and give You something to drink? And when did we see You a stranger, and invite You in, or naked, and clothe You? When did we see You sick, or in prison, and come to You?' The King will answer and say to them, 'Truly I say to you, to the extent that you did it to one of these brothers of Mine, even the least of them, you did it to Me.'

"Then He will also say to those on His left, 'Depart from Me, accursed ones, into the eternal fire which has been prepared for the devil and his angels; for I was hungry, and you gave Me nothing to eat; I was thirsty, and you gave Me nothing to drink; I was a stranger, and you did not invite Me in; naked, and you did not clothe Me; sick, and in prison, and you did not visit Me.' Then they themselves also will answer, 'Lord, when did we see You hungry, or thirsty, or a stranger, or naked, or sick, or in prison, and did not take care of You?' Then He will answer them, 'Truly I say to you, to the extent that you did not do it to one of the least of these, you did not do it to Me. Matthew 25:34-45*

How invested are we in the lives of others?

There is one who scatters, and yet increases all the more, and there is one who withholds what is justly due, and yet it results only in want. Proverbs 11:24.

Our personal desires never subside. When our flesh is stimulated, we crave more.

When is enough, enough? How do we stop feeding the beast?

We cannot be saved by deeds or having church etiquette. It's about having a heart to serve. God seeks fellowship with us. He wants sincerity. He wants our lives to impact more than us, but to reach out and touch others.

> "Is this not the fast which I choose, to loosen the bonds of wickedness, to undo the bands of the yoke, and to let the oppressed go free And break every yoke? "Is it not to divide your bread with the hungry and bring the homeless poor into the house; When you see the naked, to cover him; And not to hide yourself from your own flesh? "Then your light will break out like the dawn, and your recovery will speedily spring forth; And your righteousness will go before you; The glory of the Lord will be your rear guard. "Then you will call, and the Lord will answer; You will cry, and He will say, 'Here I am.' If you remove the yoke from your midst, the pointing of the finger and speaking wickedness. Isaiah 58:6-9

Submission to the Lord frees us of worldly temptations, just as giving of ourselves and our substance clears the channels in our prayer life. If we are obedient, we allow God to work mightily through us. Moses sacrificed his worldly position as son of Pharaoh for his eternal inheritance. Moses made a decision to choose God over his culture and what made logical sense. He saw more value in following God, and God honored him because of it.

> By faith Moses, when he had grown up, refused to be called the son of Pharaoh's daughter, choosing rather to endure ill-treatment with the people of God than to enjoy the passing pleasures of sin, considering the reproach of Christ

*greater riches than the treasures of Egypt; for he was look-
ing to the reward. Hebrews 11:24-26*

Moses could have remained in the palace, living in luxury for the
rest of his life. Instead he chose to be a Hebrew slave because he
understood the long game.

How ignorant are we to walk around with arrogance and a sense
of entitlement due to benefits that we enjoy but did nothing to
earn? If you were born into privilege, be grateful as well as humble. With privilege comes responsibility. To whom much is given,
much is also required. Those who use their position of privilege
selfishly or for evil will be judged accordingly.

Do you envy those who you consider to be born into a privileged
situation (race, social class, etc.)?

Do you despise not being born into a particular race or social class?

I believe there are benefits to not being born into certain privil-
eges. That is, if it causes dependence on God for provision. Dependence on God encourages us to walk by faith and build a relationship. That may not appear as an advantage, but when you look
at how long a human life lasts, wouldn't you rather get to know
him now?

Wouldn't you want to have a relationship with God forever, versus
temporary riches?

> *"For God so loved the world, that He gave His only begot-
> ten Son, that whoever believes in Him shall not perish, but
> have eternal life. John 3:16*

One of the richest and wisest men to ever live was Solomon. This
is his overview of money.

Whoever loves money never has enough; whoever loves wealth is never satisfied with their income. This too is meaningless. As goods increase, so do those who consume them. And what benefit are they to the owners except to feast their eyes on them? The sleep of a laborer is sweet, whether they eat little or much, but as for the rich, their abundance permits them no sleep. I have seen a grievous evil under the sun: wealth hoarded to the harm of its owners, or wealth lost through some misfortune, so that when they have children there is nothing left for them to inherit. Everyone comes naked from their mother's womb, and as everyone comes, so they depart. They take nothing from their toil that they can carry in their hands. This too is a grievous evil: As everyone comes, so they depart, and what do they gain, since they toil for the wind? All their days they eat in darkness, with great frustration, affliction and anger. This is what I have observed to be good: that it is appropriate for a person to eat, to drink and to find satisfaction in their toilsome labor under the sun during the few days of life God has given them—for this is their lot. Moreover, when God gives someone wealth and possessions, and the ability to enjoy them, to accept their lot and be happy in their toil—this is a gift of God. They seldom reflect on the days of their life, because God keeps them occupied with gladness of heart. Ecclesiastes 5:8-20

◆ ◆ ◆

Key Takeaways:

1. Ultimately, money is a tool that has no significance when we consider Heaven. Spending a lifetime chasing something that has no eternal value is useless.

2. Tomorrow is promised to no one and as soon as we take our first breath we begin to expire. Invest in your heavenly future.

3. There are rewards and crowns in heaven. Fight the good fight and finish the race.

4. It is possible to live a full life and not receive God's promise. However, your efforts will not go unrecognized or unrewarded.

5. God's Kingdom economy invests in the winning of souls. When we align ourselves with Gods interests, we position ourselves to win in the long run.

6. Beware of pride. It will push the most seasoned Christian outside of God's will.

7. God is not interested in your work, or church etiquette more than he is interested in your heart and how you treat others.

8. We are all faced with the choice of temporary riches or eternal life with God.

9. Gods way allows you to enjoy riches without compromising your soul.

CONCLUSION

God is the Creator and Source of all things on earth, and in heaven. He owns it all and gives us the power to gain wealth. We've learned that provision without the Provider's instruction is uncertain. There is potential to become obsessed with money, but we should learn to have contentment in our relationship with Christ.

We were created to work the land, but we must be careful not to chase wealth at the expense of others. Debt causes us to be slaves to our lenders and affects our relationship with God. We are expected to be good stewards of the resources God provides. He expects a return on His investment in us, for the benefit of the kingdom.

The Kingdom of God has its own economy that doesn't make sense to this world. In order to realize the freedom in Christ and the true flow of money, we must give freely as the Holy Spirit leads. By sowing, we reap much more than money itself. Money has no heavenly value. If you are wise, you will live with eternity in mind even if it means sacrificing temporal rewards.

ABOUT THE AUTHOR

Desmond A. Douglas

Desmond Douglas, is a native of Queens, New York. Growing up in the inner-city, while also fortunate enough to attend a private boarding school- New York Military Academy, Desmond was exposed to different cultures and social classes. In his late twenties, he would learn about the stock market, which is when he developed an interest in investing.

In 2005, Desmond met Regina, a young woman at Wednesday night Bible study, and by 2008 they became Mr. & Mrs. Douglas- with one son, and another on the way. Today they have three boys: Kenon, Kristion, and Korey.

Desmond is a licensed Financial Advisor with credentials that include Chartered Retirement Planning Counselor (CRPC), as well as Accredited Assets Management Specialist (AAMS). He is armed with an A.S. in Business Administration, a B.S. in Business Management & Technology, and an M.B.A. in Global Managment.

Desmond attributes his success to his faith, and undoubtedly God's grace and favor. In 2013, Desmond was ordained as a minister at Love Oasis Christian Center in Queens Village, New York.

"As a minister and financial advisor, my purpose is to educate, empower and encourage God's people. I consider this a calling, which is a privilege and an honor."

Made in the USA
Columbia, SC
20 February 2024

31838637R00071